Rising Above

LU ANN TOPOVSKI

Rising Above

DEALING WITH OUR PAST -
MAKING WAY FOR OUR FUTURE

TATE PUBLISHING
AND ENTERPRISES, LLC

Rising Above
Copyright © 2013 by Lu Ann Topovski. All rights reserved.

No part of this publication may be reproduced, stored in a retrieval system or transmitted in any way by any means, electronic, mechanical, photocopy, recording or otherwise without the prior permission of the author except as provided by USA copyright law.

Scripture quotations marked (TNIV) are taken from the *Holy Bible, Today's New International Version*®. TNIV®. Copyright © 2001, 2005 by Biblica, Inc.™ Used by permission of Zondervan. All rights reserved worldwide. www.zondervan.com

This book is designed to provide accurate and authoritative information with regard to the subject matter covered. This information is given with the understanding that neither the author nor Tate Publishing, LLC is engaged in rendering legal, professional advice. Since the details of your situation are fact dependent, you should additionally seek the services of a competent professional.

The opinions expressed by the author are not necessarily those of Tate Publishing, LLC.

Published by Tate Publishing & Enterprises, LLC
127 E. Trade Center Terrace | Mustang, Oklahoma 73064 USA
1.888.361.9473 | www.tatepublishing.com

Tate Publishing is committed to excellence in the publishing industry. The company reflects the philosophy established by the founders, based on Psalm 68:11,
"The Lord gave the word and great was the company of those who published it."

Book design copyright © 2013 by Tate Publishing, LLC. All rights reserved.
Cover design by Samson Lim
Interior design by Jake Muelle

Published in the United States of America

ISBN: 978-1-62510-314-7
1. Religion / Biblical Meditations / General
2. Religion / Christian Life / General
13.03.05

DEDICATION

This book is dedicated to my children Taylor, Spencer, and Sydney. I am grateful to God for allowing me the opportunity of motherhood, and to raise you as my own. Life is not always easy but it's worth the journey with all of you!

This book is also dedicated to the children of God who seriously desire to live out the righteousness of God in their lives. It is dedicated to those who desire to see God's holiness and kingdom work through them and around them during their lifetime here on earth.

I believe we were made to love ourselves and others but not at the risk of losing ourselves. When we have loved and lost, it takes courage to love again. This book is dedicated to those who have loved and lost. May you find the strength to love again.

Since God is love, and we are created in his image, we can trust, we can love. It's easy to love children, family, and friends. It is more of a risk to give our heart to someone who does not fit into one of these categories. At the same time, there is freedom and joy in love. It is worth our risk because we receive unspeakable joy!

Special thanks to my daughter Taylor Mason who gave me insights and helped me consider writing methods to help make this book stronger. Thanks to Antonio Otero who has supported me spiritually for years, is an awesome editor, and gifted in knowing how to operate the gifts of the Spirit in his life. Thanks to one my best friends on this earth, Lea Wiens, who experienced miracles in her life and supported me through my years of trials, and encouraged me while writing this book. Thanks to another best friend, Gail Zafiropulos, who encouraged me to write more Scripture and give more specifics in chapter two. Thank you Mika Mondragon for fresh eyes, friendship and insights. Thank you Andrea Dideon for allowing God to use you in my time of need and being there for me in my darkest hours. Thanks to my parents, Eloise Bell and George Topovski, who believed in me and helped me financially and prayerfully with this book, and loved me throughout my years of pain and trials. Lastly, thank you Tate Publishing who gave me the opportunity to publish my heart. To all of you, I will be eternally grateful!

Table of Contents

Introduction 9

Foreword................................. 13

Being on Top of Our Game 17

Knowledge and the Marriage Union........... 31

Courage to Change......................... 49

Doing Things God's Way.................... 65

Taking Responsibility...................... 77

Our Battle ... Our Victory.................. 97

Spiritual Gifts........................... 115

Love—The Bond of Perfection 127

Introduction

I originally started writing this book to those who are Christians, but had strayed from behaving like believers in Christ. As I continued writing I noticed the Spirit moving within my heart to write not only to believers who had strayed from the truth, but also to younger Christians. Then I noticed the Spirit moving within me to write to those who have been contemplating accepting Jesus as their Savior and allowing him to be their Lord.

In short, this book is written to those who are searching for answers to questions about Jesus, God, the Holy Spirit, righteousness, healing, and peace from this world. I'm not saying I have all of the answers. I don't. However, I am saying God has blessed me through my own emotional pain to learn from it and help others.

Because there has been no platform for me after graduating seminary, I continued my education and received my MBA. With the job crisis in America I was typically one out of three hundred applicants for one job. My odds were not good, and I was pushing fifty. I don't care what anyone tells you, no one wants someone with that much experience. I, too, was pushing against the goads, as was Saul. What is a 'goad,' you might ask? It is a sharp stick used to prod cattle. In other words, I was only hurting myself in not doing what I knew God was guiding me to do for him, which was finishing this book and making changes within my personal life.

I am here to teach what I have learned. My hope and prayer is for everyone to come to know Jesus Christ as their personal Savior and allow Jesus to be Lord in their lives.

By accepting Jesus as personal Savior we are given eternal life with our Heavenly Father (John 3:16) and guidance from the Holy Spirit (1 Corinthians 12:7). By allowing the Holy Spirit to guide our thoughts, words, and actions we are doing what is righteous and therefore making Jesus our Lord.

My prayers are for us as a people to choose righteousness in our lives. My hope is we seek out what it means to be a believer by reading and studying the Scriptures for ourselves, and by staying prayerful and in fellowship with our creator who desires us to call him, "Abba Father" like Jesus or in our modern day language, "Daddy."

Because music has always been a part of my life-long journey and enjoyment I have incorporated a playlist at the end of each chapter and this introduction. These playlists can be heard on both the audio version of *Rising Above* and E-Books. These songs are contemporary Christian songs you may have heard before. I have included these as well as other Christian authors throughout this book. I believe we are to be in unity as a family. As we incorporate each others' work we are in unity and therefore help everyone grow closer to each other and our Heavenly Dad. I pray the relevance of each song or recommended book will inspire you.

May the God of peace guide your thoughts and bless you as you read this book, and may the Holy

Spirit move within your life and heart so powerfully you will never be the same again.

—Lu Ann Topovski, M.Div, MBA

Playlist for Audio and E-books:

Toby Mac—Made to Love
http://www.youtube.com/watch?v=3afrg0aI350

FOREWORD

Rising Above: Dealing with Our Past, Making Way for Our Future, by Lu Ann Topovski is a book about hope. As the title implies, it is about moving forward through life's circumstances, not alone, but in the power and love of God. It is my privilege to speak good words about the book because I know its good writer, my friend and sister in Christ, whom I have known for the past nine years. Lu Ann spent an academic year in a small group I led as part of the Master of Divinity program at Ashland Theological Seminary. We not only unpacked learning's from the six classes the students took throughout the year, but spent time in personal sharing and spiritual formation. I could always count on Lu Ann for sensitivity to others, commitment to group process, raw personal honesty, but most of all for her depth of spirit. As you read these pages, you will see that these deep spiritual qualities are alive and well with their author, this multi-gifted woman of God whose holy consistency I esteem and who hold in deep Christian affection. I also know that LuAnn has had no shortage of difficult life circumstances, which make this book all the more compelling, because of the overwhelming courage and confidence she exudes through her living, life commitment to Jesus Christ.

In the introduction Lu Ann tells how the Spirit moved her to write for a broader audience than just those committed to and experienced in the Christian faith. If this book were put in the hands of someone who does not know Jesus, I think they would have a wise and practical introduction to what that Way is all about, about the life-changing difference Jesus makes, and how commitment to the fullness of his Way can make for honest and courageous, full and abundant living. She claims that she is here to teach what she has learned; knowing Lu Ann, her story and trusting the depth of her faith as I do, makes me say to you, "Listen to her!"

This is a holistic book. We are led by the author through faith, psychology, principles from spiritual formation, a keen eye for the contemporary cultural scene, and the strengths and weaknesses of the professing Christian community which are threaded throughout the eight chapters. And the book is *saturated* with scripture. This book could easily be used in a church class setting, not only because of its practicality about life, but as an introduction to scriptural living. Adam and Eve, Cain and Abel, Moses, Daniel, Jonah, Peter, and Paul inhabit these pages, how their frailties and strengths affected their relationship to God and the impact each had on their lives. Forgiveness, repentance, obedience, responsibility, the struggle with sin, discipline, change, and decision-making are just some of the large themes addressed here. But there is always a word of grace, as Lu Ann reminds us with a pastoral voice, that God deals with each of us differently, that each of us is unique, and that true intimacy with God is not just some nice wish, but a real, spiritual possibility.

She deals with the nitty-gritty issues of marriage and sex, children and family dysfunction, the generational impact of various behaviors, the imperative to seek professional help when needed and trusting and appropriating the Spirit of God in our lives. I suppose this could also be called a "Handbook on the Holy Spirit," for that holy principle, that Person of the Trinity inspires and invigorates this text. She urges us to avail ourselves of spiritual gifts analyses so we can function better in the Spirit. I love the balance of the conceptual and the practical in this book. Inspired by music herself, Lu Ann includes a playlist at the end of every chapter and acknowledges other Christian writes throughout. The book closes with a chapter on the power of love, which is always a reflection of God's love for us in Jesus Christ. She invites us to be a part of that love, quoting Romans 5:5: "Now hope does not disappoint, because the love of God has been poured into our hearts by the Holy Spirit who was given to us." Paul was right: I have never been disappointed in the hope Jesus offers; I am continually grateful to be awash in the love of God given to me through the Holy Spirit; now I am additionally grateful that Lu Ann Topovski has written a book which inspires me to celebrate this with a new fervor.

—Reverend Thomas A. Snyder
Interim Director, Master of Divinity
Cohort Program, Adjunct Faculty
Ashland Theological Seminary, Ashland, Ohio

Being on Top of Our Game

> "The Lord will make you the head, not the tail. If you pay attention to the commands of the LORD your God that I give you this day and carefully follow them, you will always be at the top, never at the bottom. Do not turn aside from any of the commands I give you today, to the right or to the left, following other gods and serving them."
>
> Deuteronomy 28:13-14

We as a human race unknowingly cooperate with our enemy and without question become oblivious to the power this enemy holds over us. We may be believers in God, but we have problems. We are called to be at the head and not the tail and yet more of us are at the tail than the head. Why?

We all have an ongoing need and desire to feel loved, to love, and to better our lives. That is partly why we go to school, church, counseling, or talk with friends about our problems. Everyone desires to have a less stressful, more manageable, and more meaningful life.

Statistics show that those of us who choose to deal honestly with our internal turmoil live longer with sincere hope, along with a more peaceful and meaningful lifestyle. Studies also show we generally have healthier bodies because we are less stressed.

Consequently we move forward in our lives and desire to be the best we can be for ourselves and our families. As we examine our hearts, we see opportunities to make changes necessary before we are reminded by our bodies or God something is not right in our life. This is our mind-body-spiritual connection.

For instance, if we have a headache it is typically due to us being stressed. The same is true about exhaustion. We give and give to others or work long and hard on a project and at some point our bodies say, "Enough!" Then we collapse. We need to rest. Our bodies cannot take it over a period of time. Stress ages us and it is unhealthy.

Resting

One of the Ten Commandments is to work six days and rest and worship on the seventh or the Sabbath. Clearly God knows better than we as to what we need in order to live a healthy, happy lifestyle. Resting and worshiping is one observation we can all benefit from. However, we frequently have something we want to get done and we get it done on Sunday, because it is typically our day off. It doesn't matter which day of the week our "Sabbath," is on. It only matters that we take one. This may be sacrilege for some, but if we think about it, many pastors take Monday or another day off during the week because they preach on Sunday.

We have all been on both sides of this issue. Our preferences should be to simply do the right thing and rest. However, our ego tells us we can get it done, or it won't hurt us to work a "bit" longer, or there is no other time to do what we need to do or we work because we get overtime pay. This does not mean to be legalistic about our day of rest. Even Jesus healed a man on the Sabbath and said to help those who are in need. In other words, use our common sense. We ultimately know internally what the right thing is to do, we have the choice to do it or not.

MAKING CHANGES

Our spiritual situation is similar. There comes a point in our lives when God tells us, "Enough!" We know we have been in the wrong about something, but we have been afraid of making changes. We have been afraid to speak up, confront, or stop sinning. We dance around our problem but we do not face it head on out of fear of rejection, being alone, not having money and the list of excuses goes on.

First Corinthians 11:31-32 speaks about the situation like this: "But if we judged ourselves, we would not come under judgment. When we are judged by the Lord, we are being disciplined so that we will not be condemned with the world."

God disciplines those he loves, (Proverbs 3:12). Many of us feel God must love us a lot! Yet when we honestly examine our hearts we know the truth. And we know when we speak the truth from our heart, we are free from guilt.

The above statement was spoken by the Apostle Paul to the Christians in Corinth advising them to examine their hearts *before* they participated in the Lord's Supper, otherwise known as communion. He said if they ate and drank in an unworthy manner, they would bring judgment to themselves. In this case an 'unworthy manner' is an impure heart, or not asking God's forgiveness for their sins before participating in the communion ceremony. He further goes on to say, "...this is why many are weak and sick, and some die."

In judging, or evaluating ourselves, we release ourselves from being judged by God. In other words, God cannot protect us from ourselves if we choose to go against his ways. We have free will. What are his ways? The simple answer is: love God, our Heavenly Father with all of our heart, soul, mind, andstrength; love our neighbor as ourself; obey the Ten Commandments; and follow the ways of Jesus.

We see those who live with no regard toward God in this world find themselves dealing with the eventual consequences of their choices. We may promise to change our ways if God forgives us this one time, or gets us out of this one mess. We need to remember, God cannot be mocked. God does not change. We change.

If we choose to ignore examination of ourselves we disregard God's ways of doing what is right and true. When we fail to make the necessary changes, we lose. In fact, the moment we think we can get away with something, is the moment we deceive ourselves. Although our ego can be strong, if we are honest and admit the truth, we are saved from the wrath of our enemy who is out to kill, steal, and destroy us (John 10:10). The power of God always overrides our spiritual enemy. The choice is always ours. The question is, how long will God let us go until he disciplines us?

This is where repentance and forgiveness come into play on everyone's part. We will not be condemned with the rest of the world when we repent of our faults and forgive ourselves and others. Ultimately, forgiveness is for our self. When we forgive someone for doing us wrong (lying, stealing, cheating, adultery) we are then released from the power that person holds over us emotionally, spiritually and subconsciously. It breaks that bond.

When we examine our hearts, ask God for forgiveness of our sins, accept Jesus as our Lord and Savior, do what is right, then we will not be destroyed with the rest of the world. Jesus promises us a life not only everlasting with him, but more than abundant here on this earth, as well (John 10:10). This is where our faith and trust in him come into play.

After our initial observation of our self, repentance of wrong, forgiveness of ourselves and others, there is an instant release of internal turmoil because at the very moment we forgive, God forgives us instantly and purifies our hearts from the unrighteous acts we have committed (1 John 1:9). The feeling of guilt is removed! That is the power of forgiveness. We may not be able to forget completely about the situation, but we can learn from it and move forward. This is God's promise to us and shows how powerful his forgiveness is towards us and how powerful our forgiveness is towards others. This is when we experience healings spiritually, emotionally and physically.

Doing what is correct in the eyes of God is the most important behavior for us in order to stay in his grace and receive his favor, not to mention, staying healthier and happier. This helps us to remain at the top and not slide down toward the tail. Do we deserve his grace and favor? No, but as our Heavenly Father, he wants to give us everything we want, just like we want to give our children what they want. This is, as we parents know, easier when we are respected and obeyed by our children.

When we choose to evade our heart's condition, we stay in internal turmoil, project our bitterness, fear, and confusion onto others. The Bible tells us, "… a cheerful heart is a good medicine but a broken spirit dries up our bones" (Proverbs 17:22). When our heart convicts us we do not have a happy heart. On the contrary, we have high blood pressure, headaches, and other problems. We do not live a full life because we cannot physically or mentally do what we want because of our ailments which came from our unhappy heart.

We could buy into a false belief or lie that we have gone too far and can't make things right. In a way we are correct, we can't make it right. But God can. He wants to make things better for all of us. It is we who need to take the first step and admit we are wrong. Just like in Alcoholics Anonymous or any ten-step program, the first step is to admit "I am an alcoholic." It is never too late. Ask any counselor, pastor, or true friend. Life is worth living, especially with those in whom we love.

When we choose to look at the root causes of our struggles, we find pain and hurt which has been carried, sometimes for years. This pain could be caused by a sin we have committed or a wrongful act committed against us. In some cases it is a combination of the two because bitterness is carried by the one who was sinned against. When this happens we tend to project our pain onto another person. This is how cycles continue. The other obstacle for us is that we unfortunately can carry sins from our ancestors, which is known as generational sin (Exodus 20:5).

When we choose to look at and work through *our* feelings and heart issues, we have a more peaceful heart and more stable mind. Forgiving ourselves and others is the most common denominator which gives us the peace we desire. We simply are able to continue with our life, instead of living in the pain from our past.

Letting Go

We see many Christian's turn away from what the Bible says—forgive others or admit our wrongs. Sadly, some Christian's lack desire to do the will of God if it means admitting wrongs committed. This is especially true if by admittance we would need to give up status, material objects, or an addiction. Pride ultimately is the culprit. We don't want to lose face or feel like an impostor in the eyes of others. We have shame. So we hide by not telling the truth. A cowardly act usually rooted in a learned behavior from our childhood. But just like everything else, with Jesus there is hope. Dr. Terry Wardle from Ashland Theological Seminary and founder of Healing Care Ministries speaks candidly about these issues in several of his books: *Draw Close to the Fire*, *Wounded*, and *Transforming Path*. If we as believers cannot manifest the simple foundations of being a Christian, then how are we going to manifest the power of God in our lives? If we know the truth, but don't do our part, we are not going to be free. We find sometimes our prideful ego is greater than the reverence and respect we show toward God. We therefore are not acting like Christians. If this is the case, we are too entrenched within our own lives, false beliefs or pain. We are, as Pastor Dean Fulks from Life Point church says, "Impostors masquerading as children of God." We are lost in our own world.

We read in John chapter eight about a woman caught in the act of adultery. As the teachers of the law continued to badger Jesus as to what to do with this woman, Jesus finally said, "He who is without sin could cast the first stone." As they all began walking away because of the conviction in their own hearts, Jesus said to her, "Woman, where are those accusers of yours? Has no one condemned you?" She said, "No one, Lord." And Jesus said to her, "Neither do I condemn you; go and sin no more" (John 8:10-11).

If we are to be like Jesus, if we are really "children of God" we too ought not condemn or judge others. This is not easy given the condition of our world today because condemning and judging others is the mind-set of our human race. Even though we may like what Jesus said to her, "Neither do I condemn you; go and sin no more." The part we sometimes miss is the "go and sin no more."

Stop Making Excuses

Once we are born again and have asked Jesus to forgive us of our sins, we are told by him to, "go and sin no more."

This is where we 'judge ourselves' in every thought, word, deed, and gesture. This is not to necessarily micro-manage ourselves but rather, keep ourselves in check. If something is not right, we make the change. And as we continue to do what is right in God's eyes, he will bless our situation. This is our freedom. It feels good to be ourselves without judgment and learn life skills as we go. We need to lighten up on ourselves and others so we don't feel we are under a microscope. At the same time, we need to know the facts of how life works so we can improve upon our internal joy and long term happiness.

Unfortunately, many of us Christians are not forgiving each other, which is a sin. We hate and gossip about each other, which are sins. Some of us are doing what we know is wrong in the eyes of God, which is open rebellion toward him. Our lists of transgressions go on and on. If this is the case, we are probably miserable.

If our focus is on revenge, bitterness, and avoidance rather than on God's love and forgiveness, we have problems being a Christian. If that is the case we are fence riders. We may believe enough to accept Jesus as our Savior, but we do not want to take actions to show he is our Lord. We like to take control of our own lives and do not trust our creator.

This control issue brings on anxiety, arguments and ultimate dissatisfaction because the rage on the inside is being projected onto others in a way in which is believed to be righteous anger. Yet it is very unhealthy. We hide behind blaming others instead of accepting responsibility for the way God is guiding us.

Saul, before he became the Apostle Paul, had a similar dilemma. While he was on his way to Damascus to persecute Christians, Jesus met him along the way and said to him, "Saul, Saul, why do you persecute me? It is hard for you to kick against the goads" (Acts 26:14). Remember, a goad was a sharp stick used to prod cattle. The New Living Translation says it this way, "it is useless for you to fight against my will." So Jesus was saying, "You can't fight against me. When you hurt me or my people, you are only hurting yourself."

Taking the Steps

The only way for us to be everything we have been created to be is to be honest with God, and do his will. How do we do this? By first admitting we have been wrong, and perhaps have ignored his call; that we missed the mark (are sinners). Next, we ask God to forgive us. This includes after our salvation because we are not perfect. We still make mistakes. We have a learning curve but understandably, it's not to be taken advantage of or manipulated. After our heartfelt repentance, we are then forgiven by our creator, the God of heaven and earth.

When we believe God loves us with an everlasting love, by trusting his ways in that we do what he asks, we open doors to our peace, healing, and our freedom in Christ. Our advocate, Jesus Christ the only righteous person, shed his blood for us to make this possible. His shed blood blots out our sins when we ask God for forgiveness. Now, as the children of God, we no longer want to live in darkness "because the love of God has been poured into our hearts by the Holy Spirit" (Romans 5:5). This is why we bring our issues into the light, making it possible for us to be freed from them.

As we allow conviction in our hearts, we make the necessary changes in our lives. Our hearts then no longer condemn us and we feel freedom to be ourselves again! What does that mean? It means we no longer feel guilt or shame because we feel the release and accept our forgiveness.

What happens if we do not make the necessary changes? We hold our entire being (body, soul, heart, and mind) captive, simply because we choose to hold on to our old ways and past hurts. No one said this Christian life was going to be easy, but this is how it is done for our freedom's sake. Will we fail at times? Yes, but we are all worth it. When one of us is hurting, we all suffer at some level from the pain. When we help ourselves, we are helping others because we are all part of the body of Christ.

Receiving

Simply put, if we have internal turmoil, we have unresolved issues which prohibit us from being everything we have been created to be or do. Sin prohibits us from receiving all of God's blessings. We as Christians are missing out on blessings because we lack Scriptural knowledge and understanding about sin. We too often rely on others to teach us, but we as Christians have the responsibility to learn and read the Bible for ourselves. It's not hard, in fact, it's quite easy. Second Timothy 2:15 says, "Be diligent to present yourself approved to God, a worker who does not need to be ashamed, rightly dividing the word of truth."

As we take the time to know God by reading and studying the Bible, we learn about his will for us. It's easier to make decisions because we are more discerning of right from wrong. We learn what it means to be a child of God. We show ourselves approved by God as we believe and therefore do what the Bible tells us. As we do what the Bible says, we know, and can feel, we are in right standing with Him because there is a relationship not just an idol worship. We have a peace within us which enables us to have patience through difficult situations, or at least know to have patience in inconceivable and heartbreaking times.

Hebrews 4:12 says, "For the word of God is living and active. Sharper than any double-edged sword, it penetrates even to dividing soul and spirit, joints and marrow; it judges the thoughts and attitudes of the heart." This Scripture informs us the Bible penetrates through our entire being: soul, spirit, body, and heart. Now that is powerful!

When we know God is love and he created us in his image it is easier to allow ourselves to love, forgive, and love again. As we learn to love God and ourselves we desire to do things his way. We appreciate the fact he loved us enough to create us. As we become more grateful and appreciative of who we are in him, the greater our desire grows to be workers united with God (2 Corinthians 6:1). We become known as children of God.

As we do what we know is right by God's standards, whether we want to or not, we are rising above our thoughts and old behaviors. We are allowing God to work through us and guide us through our situations. As we rise above and deal with these situations the way God desires, we are acting like his kids. We are honorable in his sight. We will therefore, receive his favor, blessings and protection.

"His ways are everlasting," as Habakkuk 3:6 says. We feel this, we know this to be true, and it is verified by our sense of peace, our blessings and our personal relationship with him and others. There is literally no other relationship more powerful or loving than the one we can have with him. He wants to show us how much he loves us. He wants to show us that he is the way, the truth and the life. If we truly desire to know Jesus, our Savior and Lord we must trust his ways will override our ways. When we have faith and trust his ways we are following him. We are allowing him to work through us. We are able to manifest the Kingdom of God on earth in our lives.

Audio and E-books Playlist Chapter 1

Tenth Avenue North—You Are More
http://www.youtube.com/watch?v=IwtcwQwgdsA

Kutless—What Faith Can Do
http://www.dailymotion.com/video/xct9tr_kutless-what-faith-can-do-official_music#.URa7mqU0WSo

Barlow Girl—Never Alone
http://www.youtube.com/watch?v=x8QubLxJI54

Newsboys—Born Again
http://www.youtube.com/watch?v=VHcCBtIcxhQ

QUESTIONS FOR CHAPTER 1

1. Have you made a bad choice, a mistake, in your life that keeps bothering you?
2. Can you ask God to forgive you for that mistake?
3. Can you forgive yourself?
4. Is there someone who has hurt you in the past?
5. Does the pain of that hurt hinder you from moving forward in your life?
6. Is it possible for you to forgive that person right now?
7. If you cannot forgive in this moment, is there a person or a counselor you can talk with to help you work through the pain?
8. Can you forgive yourself for any bitterness you have held toward that person?
9. Where do you see yourself one year from now? Five years from now? What steps can you take to reach your goals?

Knowledge and the Marriage Union

> "My people are destroyed from lack of knowledge. Because you have rejected knowledge, I also reject you as my priests."
>
> Hosea 4:6a

> "Apply your heart to instruction and your ears to words of knowledge."
>
> Proverbs 23:12

The first line of this Scripture, "My people are destroyed from lack of knowledge" is profound. The New International Readers Version says it this way, "My people are destroyed because they don't know me." This could be our wake-up call. We have heard it said, "Knowledge is power." But what if we don't know what to do with knowledge or ignore it altogether? In the original Hebrew text, God is saying, "My people do not know me intimately and therefore, our relationship is destroyed." Because we refuse God's knowledge, intimacy with God is lost. We see a similar correlation within some marriages today where intimacy has been lost through multitude of layers of secrets and silence. Therefore, we in turn lose each other, and intimacy is lost. We feel alone and look for other ways to fulfill our desire to love and be loved. We feel as if we are left to fend for ourselves because our intimacy is gone.

QUESTIONING

One would think we would desire to know God because we don't want to be destroyed. But these days, that's not how we think. We question. Very few of us want to take responsibility for anything we have done wrong, including and especially with infidelity. We have learned to manipulate, shift blame, and dance around our situations, even when we know, but may not believe, "the truth will set us free" (John 8:32).

As believers in Jesus Christ our spiritual reality is we are God's chosen people along with the Israelites (Ephesians 3). We are called Christian's because just as Jesus Christ had the Holy Spirit working through him, we too as believers in Christ have the same Holy Spirit working through us to do good, and to oppose evil. Colossians 1:27-28 says it like this, "...to them God has chosen to make known among the Gentiles (non-Jewish people) the glorious riches of this mystery, which is Christ in you the hope of glory. We proclaim him, admonishing, and teaching everyone with all wisdom so that we may present everyone fully mature in Christ."

As Christian's we have priests, pastors and other ministry leaders to instruct us in the proper Christian ways. In other words, to help us mature in Christ. But as we look around we see a lot of immature Christians. We may be one of them. We have some leaders in the church, as we all know, who have failed us and have brought negative association onto Christianity. Those of us who are Christians but not in ministry per se' are also priests (Revelation 1:6) of the one true God.

In the Old Testament priests upheld the Ten Commandments and spoke the laws to Israel, to whom were God's chosen people otherwise known as Jewish people, or Jews. Now we are one people under this umbrella. However, we as everyday Christians have failed to uphold the ways of God, just as the priests failed in Hosea's time. The priests in Hosea's time were not only allowing prostitution, they were prostituting themselves with male and female prostitutes.

Not so much has changed in this generation. We still hear of those who have done the same as the priests in Hosea's time, abusing their power for their own sexual desires. Unfortunately, we have not heard enough about Christians who are sold out to God and have prayed for God to take their lives before they would sin against their spouses, families or church. These are ordinary men and women of God who fight through everyday temptations with the power of the Holy Spirit and understanding of God. These are our true heroes and heroines who may not work a day in a church building but live their lives out loud with conviction. Are they perfect? No! But they are a lot of fun to be with because they do not care that others may judge them. Their judge is the Lord.

Some Issues

Some churches may only address spiritual issues. They don't necessarily want to cross over the line of church and state, deal with sexual issues of our day, or confront their own traditions. It's unfortunate we don't hear enough about our physical bodies or mental abilities but mainly the spiritual meaning of being a Christian. Spiritual understanding is imperative, yet we also have a body and mind we need to keep in check. In fact, as Christians, our bodies are temples of the Holy Spirit and we are called to honor God with our bodies rather than use them for sexual immorality or hurt them in any way (1 Corinthians 6, Galatians 5).

We wonder sometimes if we don't hear enough about this because the traditional church does not know how to address it or because of it having its own issues, or fears of being judged. Regardless, we as the body of Christ need to have a good understanding so we can make healthy and knowledgeable decisions.

First Corinthians 6:18-20 says, "Flee from sexual immorality. All other sins people commit are outside their bodies but those who sin sexually sin against their own bodies. Do you not know that your bodies are temples of the Holy Spirit, who is in you, whom you have received from God? You are not your own; you were bought at a price. Therefore honor God with your bodies."

Just as in Hosea's and Noah's time, or in the time of the cities of Sodom and Gomorrah or the Corinthians' time, we today still have the same issues in our society. Why? Sex was created by God and is good. But anything good can be perverted. Perversion is taking something good and twisting or turning it into something other than its original purpose.

Sex is a basic desire and some believe a human need. It was created by God originally for pro-creation. At the same time, God made it pleasurable. We are all called to marry if we have this sexual desire so it can remain sacred between a man and a woman within their marriage union. But some traditional churches prefer not to talk about sex. This is a problem because we as human beings find other human beings attractive and desirable. Sex is natural and needs to be addressed, understood, and respected.

It is critical to choose the right mate who will be faithful sexually. Why? Within the sexual act you become one flesh, one union. This is a spiritual connection not just an emotional and physical connection. It is beautiful. It's important to marry someone like-minded in our beliefs so there are no problems with this later, but it is equally important to marry for love and friendship.

Sex is part of the love shared with our spouse, our soul-mate, and it is good. It is love making, and making love. This courtship is what helps keep the marriage from breakdown and corrosion. If we are taught otherwise then one of the partners may leave to get their emotional and sexual needs met elsewhere. Perhaps it would behoove us as the body of Christ to read Solomon's Song of Songs as it speaks beautifully about a man and woman's intimacy and love for one other. It speaks poetically and passionately of ecstasy and eroticism. It is the most passionate book within the Bible in regard to being in love with another human being. Just as within Song of Songs, we ought not be ashamed of our reverence, passion, and intimacy with our lover. We ought to embrace this gift.

If we love someone, we want to please them. Erotic love making and orgasms are part of our experience of making love together. Erotic simply means giving sexual pleasure or sexually arousing. If we love each other, we want to please each other. This is love. This is good. We may think it absurd to speak about such things in a Christian book but as we read in Song of Songs, it is not new. It is beautiful.

If we are keeping our love-making sacred at home there is typically no problem in our marriage union. Our desire is for the one at home who loves us and in whom we love. It strengthens our marriage and love for one another.

Strengthening Our Marriage Covenant

It takes both parties to make a marriage work whether we are in or out of the bedroom. It takes team work in the household chores, dealing with money issues and children. If we are not able to work well outside of the bedroom then it is easier to fall out of love. Falling in love is not our problem, it is staying in love. If we are not willing to take intimacy with our spouse seriously throughout our marriage it is likely we become part of the many statistics.

The divorce rate in America is staggering. Fifty percent of first marriages end in divorce; 67 percent of second marriages divorce and; 74 percent of third marriages divorce (Jennifer Baker of the Forest Institute of Professional Psychology in Springfield, Missouri). Even though the combined average divorce rate in America is approximately 65 percent, we cannot tell the difference between Christians and non-Christians because most have had extra-marital affairs. In the 35 percent of marriages which stay together, the common denominator for those who are Christians is that 99 percent of them pray together for the same things.

The question then becomes, do we want to pray together? If we begin praying during our courtship then we have already made a foundational choice to keep God first, and our love strong in our relationship. This doesn't mean those who are married currently can't start praying together. On the contrary, it means if we are married the statistics are high enough to indicate that if we want to stay together we want to incorporate prayer into our daily lives.

When we as a marriage partnership go together as one vertically to our creator, we have a stronger chance of staying on the same page throughout each day and ultimately our lifetime. This is because we, as a team, are strengthening our spiritual relationship with our creator and with each other. When we pray, "strengthen our love for each other Lord" then our love is strengthened. It is powerful. It is beautiful.

Our relationship with each other is vital. We all need to feel loved by our spouse. By saying we love each other, giving hugs, kisses, leaving notes, buying gifts and by being sexual regularly help to keep the love and relationship alive and well. If both partners are communicating and doing their best in these areas then faithfulness comes naturally.

This may be where some of us as Christians fail—by not communicating our love language to one another. This is sometimes due to our personal weaknesses in self-control and lack of understanding in the ramifications of our actions. We also need to take into account outside influences we have in our life. It is crucial we keep ourselves out of situations we know will tempt us. We have a responsibility to each other to put ourselves in situations which support protection of our union and future goals. We all could use a little more strength to make the right choices for ourselves and ultimately for our family.

If we could get the marriage part down and be good examples for our children we would be on the brink of turning this downfall of the human race around. When we first get married we are blinded by our love and cannot foresee problems in our future. Then problems, temptations, children, and jobs fog our thinking of the one we fell in love with and promised everything to. When this starts to happen we need to talk to our spouse, see a counselor, or read a good book on marriage. I recommend, *The 5 Love Languages*, by Gary Chapman. It's an excellent book before and throughout any marriage.

It is vital we listen to and communicate with our spouse about observations, thoughts, and feelings. If we begin to speak to the opposite sex about our personal problems within our marriage it creates a temptation for both parties. If this ever happens to us we need to stop. If an unhappy spouse of the opposite sex is confiding in us, we need to remind the unhappy spouse to talk with their spouse or a counselor. We need to be accountable for our thoughts and feelings, not avoid them. Looking for someone other than our spouse to comfort us is a cowardly act. We can face our problems head on, and when we do, we move forward in freedom. It is imperative we do whatever is necessary to keep our love for each other alive. We have to remember our love is worth the effort. It takes two. We need to do our part in not letting our love die.

Know this, no matter what the situation, there is hope if both parties are willing. As we repent, and forgive, we can move on victoriously. As we become aware of the importance of being honest and keeping God's laws we can make better choices for our self and our family. As we allow God to guide us through our circumstances, generational cycles will be severed.

Unfortunate Realities

On the other hand, if one spouse chooses to no longer be faithful sexually or honest about infidelity, we are no longer spiritually bound to them or their lies. It is time to walk away from them and their fantasy world because the only thing holding this marriage together is the legal documentation. Trust was broken. Intimacy is severed. When this is the case there are usually arguments and disagreements which cause more chaos. Jesus said, "Every kingdom divided against itself will be ruined, and every city or household divided against itself will not stand" (Matthew 12:25).

If this marriage is broken and only one spouse wants it healed, it will not work. It is divided and cannot stand. If the marriage stays together for the sake of the children it is likely the children will grow up feeling alone in a dysfunctional atmosphere. Because there is a lack of agreement between the parents, the children will eventually disrespect both parents and make their own decisions. Those decisions are not always good. The entire family system is dysfunctional. There are usually disagreements as to how to raise the children, there is a lack of love, and disrespect is typically modeled. It is best for us to protect our self and our children and end the marriage.

This is unfortunate as no one wants to be a statistic. But no one should stay in this type of marriage due to tradition, fear, or what someone else might think. We Christians have historically stayed together because we thought it was the right thing to do. This is a false belief. We may pray and believe and trust things will change. But they don't if one spouse is not in it for the right reason, love. This method clearly does not work. There is more heartache and time wasted on someone who does not want to take responsibility, love or change.

We know what time it is in our heart when there is no love or trust in our marriage. We feel it because we have been one flesh and when adultery is introduced into the marriage we feel our union severed by another. We no longer feel supported in the things we desire and if we believe one lie, other lies follow. This is not freedom in a marriage. This is bondage.

When this is the case it is good to be courageous and move on so we can fulfill our own dreams and calling. At some point we have to believe in ourselves enough to get out of the relationship which is only a marriage due to the legal documentation. We must realize the marriage union itself is dead.

Again, when children are involved this makes the situation more complicated. We may wonder if we should stay together for the children but this model of marriage does not work. The children will recycle the learned behavior. It is best to sever the relationship so the children learn it is not okay to abuse or be abused. They learn instead it is okay to protect themselves and do what is right even if it is difficult.

To drive this home just a little further, if we are asked to believe a lie in a marriage, it is manipulative. In a sense one of the spouses is turning away from God as they turn away from the marriage covenant. The Bible tells us the father of lies is the devil (John 8:44). So when we are asked to believe a lie we are not sharing the same beliefs.

Second Corinthians 6 states being unequal in our beliefs this way:

> Do not be yoked together with unbelievers. For what do righteousness and wickedness have in common? Or what fellowship can light have with darkness? What harmony is there between Christ and Belial? What does a believer have in common with an unbeliever? What agreement

is there between the temple of God and idols?
For we are the temple of the living God.

> (2 Corinthians 6:14-16a)

This may sound harsh but if we do our part and pray, and if our spouse chooses to continue their ungodly behavior and not honor our marriage covenant, we are released from them spiritually. We cannot allow fear, our pride, or shame discourage us in what is best for our future. This is unfortunate but no one should stay in an abusive marriage. Lying and manipulation is just as abusive as verbal, sexual, or physical abuse. No one should stay due to tradition, fear of being alone or what someone else might think.

One of the reasons Moses wrote a divorce decree was, "… because men's hearts were hardened" toward their spouses (Mark 10:5). Even in Moses's time, some men would marry a woman and accept the dowry (inheritance) of their wife. Then if they did not like their wife, they would divorce them. They kept the dowry and the woman had to either go back to her family, work, or get kicked out on the streets. Some became prostitutes because they felt it was the only way to survive.

We still see this today in modern day society. Why do we see this? We see this because men's (and women's) hearts are hard. If we don't get our way, we throw a temper tantrum or leave the marriage physically or emotionally instead of talking out the problem. Traditional churches enable this behavior more commonly in men because it is hammered in our heads that the man is the head of the household. The husband gets the final say. But that is not how marriage was set up originally with Adam and Eve. Originally, they became one flesh through intercourse, they were not ashamed of their nakedness and they were to rule over the earth equally together. After they sinned against God by doing what he asked them not to do, they were under a new law where the husband would rule over his wife (Genesis 1-3). When Jesus came to earth, died for our sins, rose from the dead, and ascended to the right hand of God, he broke that law. Therefore, marriage is no longer under that law (Galatians 3:28).

Again, when children are involved this makes the situation more complicated. We may feel it is best to stay together for the children but this model of marriage does not work. The children will recycle the learned behavior. It is best to sever the relationship so the children learn it is not okay to abuse or be abused. We as a church cannot continue to enable this behavior. Accountability is the key. On the other hand, when abusive marriages are severed, children learn there is strength in doing what is right. They will not have fear, but rather strength, to do what is right for themselves in their future situations.

Back to Hosea

So what does the marriage union have to do with Hosea? Hosea 4:6 is very austere as is the entire book of Hosea. Hosea was a prophet who was told by God to marry a prostitute. At first she was faithful but she later left Hosea for her previous lifestyle of other lovers.

God told Hosea to buy her back. After his wife, Gomer, returned fully reconciled, there was no mention of her leaving him again.

Hosea's life was a metaphor and symbolization of Israel during that time period. Israel left God's ways for other ways of the world—other lovers. The book of Hosea portrays God's constant and persistent love for his own people. After Israel returned to God through their repentance, God blessed them again. God forgave them of their acting out and God forgives us. His desire is for us to return to him and his love for us.

When we read, "My people" are destroyed for a lack of knowledge, 'My people' indicates those who were Israelites. In other words, God's chosen people. We as Christians are also God's chosen people. The book of Hosea shows the status quo of God's people, including priests, of that time period. We see a direct correlation between God's chosen people then and God's chosen people now. We are being destroyed, perhaps paralyzed in that we do not know what to do with our lives and marriages are falling apart. We could blame our spiritual leadership because we all know it all "starts from the top" with our lack of understanding between what is right and wrong. But at some point we all need to take responsibility for our own decisions.

For those of us who do know the difference yet ignore it, we see we are without God's fullest blessings in our lives, as are our children. Some of our lives are in shambles. We feel it and we may wonder why? Some of us may know why. Yet according to Hosea, we are destroyed because we lack intimacy with God—or ignore his ways. We may know the truth, and know it sets us free but we deny the truth because of our own agenda, fears or personal issues. The choice to change is ours.

As we choose to make positive changes back to God in our individual lives it filters over into our marriage union. We therefore become better lovers because we are more respectful of ourselves, our spouse and others. We are evolving into who we were originally created to be and we therefore are better equipped in understanding and fulfilling our purpose (Jeremiah 29:11).

Proverbs 1:7 says, "The fear of the LORD is the beginning of knowledge, but fools despise wisdom and discipline."

If we do not understand or have knowledge of God, it is one thing but to despise it makes us fools. We might know about God or we may have heard about Jesus, but without the understanding of God, we cannot have a relationship with him. Some say ignorance is bliss. Yet if we choose to stay ignorant it leads to our early demise.

This Scripture from Hosea tells us we are destroyed two different ways. First, we are destroyed for our *lack* of knowledge. Second, we are also destroyed for our *rejection* of knowledge. We may know the right thing to say or do but we choose not to do it out of fear, selfishness, or some other reason. As we make choices diametrically opposed to the truth, we choose to turn our face from truth. We allow fear, arrogance, or pride to set into our lives. We then allow it to take over. We turn our face toward what we know is unacceptable, (especially if it were done to us), and choose to do it anyway.

We care less about consequences to our choices, and allow our desire or opinion of other's rank higher. We think we can handle the consequences and this is where our internal destruction begins. Pride comes before we fall on our face. (Proverbs 16:18) This has been the same since the beginning of the fall with Lucifer, who is now our arch enemy who only wants us to feel pain and ultimately lose our soul to him in the end.

We were designed to have a relationship with our Heavenly Father, our *Abba* Father which translates into *Daddy*. However, for some of us we have either a superficial relationship with him; or perhaps no relationship at all because we've rejected his ways. We have been given the Bible as our manuscript for life. Maybe if it were entitled "Life Manual for Dummies" it might spark our interest.

If we ignore or reject what the Bible says, or parts of it, we miss out on what our Heavenly Dad wants us to know about ourselves, him, and the spiritual battle we all face. Do we understand all that we read? Not always, but that is why we talk to a trusted pastor or friend who reads and understands the Bible. Or, we could go directly to God and ask him to reveal a mystery to us, or give us a Scripture passage to help us in our situation. He is known for giving direction when asked and is still capable of doing so. He wants us to ask and trust him. It is we who need to trust him when we ask.

By denying the Bible or part of it we forfeit a more complete, and intimate, relationship with our creator. Let's face it. He created us for a reason. He created us because he wants a relationship with us and because he has a purpose for each of us. So it is up to us to see how this works and test his ways to see what happens. When we at least test out his promises and ways we can then give a true assessment. If he loved us enough to create us, he loves us enough to know how to keep us happy. But just as in any marriage union, we have to be faithful in order to feel the peace and joy. We need to trust our Lord and his ways.

Audio and E-books Playlist Chapter 2

Steven C. Chapman—How Do I Love Her?
http://www.youtube.com/watch?v=2eFJqyzKrNs

Sanctus Real—Lead Me
http://www.youtube.com/watch?v=yLr6G8Xy5uc

Rebecca St. James—Wait For Me
http://www.youtube.com/watch?v=YyoVIvyHnw8

Toby Mac—Family
http://www.youtube.com/watch?v=JVG4vPPHu7c

Questions for chapter 2

1. Do you have an intimate relationship with God?
2. Do you feel you know God or know about him?
3. What are some ways you could grow more intimate with God
4. If you are married, how is your intimate relationship with your spouse?
5. How can you grow closer together emotionally?
6. How can you be more intimate?

7. How can you ask for what you need, inside and outside of the bedroom?
8. Can you give what your spouse asks of you?
9. Are you in an abusive marriage? If so, what steps can you take to help yourself and your children?

Courage to Change

"because you have ignored the law of your God,
I also will ignore your children."

Hosea 4:6b

As workers together with God (2 Corinthians 6:1), we were created to have an intimate relationship with him and others. When we have intimacy with God, we trust in his ways and enjoy walking in them. Our plans could be his plans and when they are, he so graciously gives us *all* of the desires of our heart as we continue to obey his ways. In fact, the more intimate we can be with God, the more intimate we can be with our spouse. Now that is worth fighting for!

Yet we as a human race in general want things instantly when we ask for them. So, when we ask God for something and it doesn't arrive on our doorstep in fifteen minutes or less we are disappointed. Sometimes we have temper tantrums, and often try to do things our own way. This is where we fail.

We as a human race, or at least in America, have unlearned patience. It's kind of like going through a drive-through and ordering fast food. We want things instantly. Yet studies show it takes approximately thirty days to change a habit, as we make the conscious effort to change the habit. After establishing the habit, it becomes more natural. Then it takes another approximate sixty days to build upon that habit to produce our character trait. This is true for any behavior, positive or negative. So if we want to test God's promises we could focus on one of his promises for ninety days and then judge for ourselves. Why ninety days? Three months, or ninety days, formulates our identity.

We may know about the God of Israel who created the heavens and earth, parted the Red Sea, saved Daniel in the lion's den, and sent his only begotten son to save us. Yet we don't always acknowledge him because we sometimes have a mental discomfort with his ways and how long they take. Or we don't really believe he will help us. We know we should trust his ways even if we don't understand them. We know by keeping his laws, truth is revealed to us, and we are then enabled to teach others, even if it is by example. It is the waiting part that drives us all crazy!

Homework That Helps

If we were to print out or write down the Ten Commandments for example, and read them every day for three months, we would begin to see how God's promises begin to affect our thinking and behavior. If during this three month time period we were to choose one commandment to focus on like commandment nine, "thou shall not lie," and practice it, we could change a character trait. Now that is life changing.

Just telling the truth or avoiding falseness may be a challenge in itself for some of us, but it's a start. If nothing else, by telling the truth we won't feel the guilt we had when we would have told a lie in the same situation three months earlier. That in itself is a stress reliever. That is progress.

As we know, when we reject God or his ways, we distance ourselves from having an honest and intimate relationship with him and others. The way we view and respect God is the way we will view and respect others. We have to acknowledge we cannot get into a right relationship with God or others by the world's standards. We can, however, have an honest and real relationship with him and others by his standards. The only way to know his standards is through his Scriptures, then to live them out in our daily lives. As we do this we won't be surprised by our new standards. We begin desiring to be around people whom we respect and people who respect us. It is a natural transition.

As mentioned previously, we have all missed the mark and sinned at some point in our lives, so we are not alone. We have lots of company. The most crucial thing is to simply turn back around and run toward our Dad in heaven, not away from him. Know this—that is exactly what God wants most from all of us, just like if our child left us and then returned home. Our human nature is either fight or flight. When we fight, we go back home to God who created us and deal with the consequences. When we are in flight mode, we run in the other direction which will only bring more heartache and no healing. Know this, our courage to change will change not only the direction of our life, but the world around us. We therefore leave this world in a better place than when we found it.

Isaiah 53:6 says, "We all, like sheep, have gone astray, each of us has turned to his own way; and the Lord has laid on him (Jesus) the iniquity of us all."

This Scripture is true for us today. We have all gone our own way. We have forsaken what we used to hold dear to our hearts. So how do we come back to God, and stay close to those in whom we love? We first need to acknowledge we did something wrong. Then make the choice to ask for forgiveness. It would be advantageous for us to read the Scriptures, so we increase our dependence on our Lord, by trusting his ways. People don't typically want to read the Bible, but it helps! It is our owner's manual and by reading it we receive instructions, discernment, and a desire to do what is right. It strengthens our faith. It feels good and brings us joy and peace when we act out what we believe is true.

Romans 10:17 says, "So then faith comes by hearing, and hearing by the word of God."

If we indeed were created in God's image, as Genesis 1: 26-27 states, it would only make sense we read what our creator has given us along with understanding our historical ancestry. When we stop reading his Word, we begin to forget to practice what we know to be true. It is like anything we learn in school, if we don't use it, we most commonly lose it. We begin to compromise. We then make shaky decisions. We believe our own lies, or think we can get away with them. We turn our face from God.

When we no longer practice what we know, our faith is weakened. We begin to slip away from the truth, and then we begin to make decisions we know are wrong and eventually regret. We are not clear on what is right, and we think what we do will not harm us or others. We believe we are above the laws of God. We are deceived. We eat the whole denial pill.

Our discernment is weakened and decisions are harder to make. Eventually, we begin making poorer choices, which are seeds sown into our future and into the future of our children. Then, we begin to hide behind our lies. When this happens we have fallen into our own addiction. Addictions are strongholds which are very difficult to get out from. Addictions can be drugs, alcohol, lying, gambling, sex, shopping, or anything that takes us away from ourselves and our creator. It is something we can no longer control. The addiction controls us. When we fall this far we need to recognize we can't do it on our own. We need to ask for help.

Who We Struggle Against

As Christians and especially as a family, we need to realize this life we live is a spiritual battle, and we have an enemy. Ephesians 6:10-12 says it like this, "Finally, be strong in the Lord and in his mighty power. Put on the full armor of God so that you can take your stand against the devil's schemes. For our struggle is not against flesh and blood, but against the rulers, against the authorities, against the powers of this dark world and against the spiritual forces of evil in the heavenly realms." Our enemy is the same enemy as our creator's. Our enemy is very clever and he unfortunately knows our nature very well. In fact, our sinful nature is his nature. He will begin to tempt us with our own desires and make sin look very inviting so we do what Adam and Eve did in the Garden of Eden, and rebel against God. We may not think of it as rebelling against God; we think of it as simply doing what we *want*. We have all heard it said, "If it feels good, do it." As we begin this pattern in our lives we become 'forgetful hearers' as James 1:25 tells us.

When we make a conscious decision to do what we know is against God and his ways, we are rebelling against him. We are flipping him off—giving him the middle finger. This may sound harsh, but it is true.

All of our life is made up of choices. How can we make good choices if we don't respect what is right. When we do know right from wrong the Bible tells us it's better to not have known what was right than to know and still do what is wrong. After we do what we know is wrong, we open ourselves to enemy territory. We open ourselves to our rival and to his deceptive ways. This happens just by choosing to do what we know is wrong.

We may have pleasure in the moment but we later suffer the consequences of our sins, along with guilt, shame, and distance between those we love. If we don't change our ways they become strongholds. False beliefs of thinking set in, and we again begin to believe another lie. Because of pride, we sometimes feel we do not need to, nor want to, repent. We become more distant from God and others. Then we become loners. Our discernment between good and evil is weakened or we simply don't care anymore. Without a repenting heart, we have growing guilt, fear, and bitterness, not to mention more distance between those whom we have sinned against and once loved.

The consequences to our sins afflict our heart even more. More importantly, our children are affected. Our children are extensions of us. They are the human race of the future. What we think, say, and do will affect their future. We model life for them and our actions are learned behaviors growing deep within the souls of our children. If we are righteous, they will learn righteousness. If we are unrighteous, they will learn unrighteousness from us. When we have false beliefs, they learn false beliefs. If we are prejudice they will likely be prejudice as well. Ultimately, we are responsible to God for ourselves and our children.

Hosea 4:6b says, "… because you have ignored the law of your God, I also will ignore your children." This part of Scripture is a Herculean task *we* put on our children, should we decide to intentionally ignore God, and decide to handle a situation our own way. As we take an assiduous look at the bigger picture of our past and take responsibility for our actions, we see which way our past decisions have led us.

As we look back on our lives, we see the manifestations of our decisions in the lives of our children. If we are born again believers, and if we believe the Bible is true, and have done the best we could to model it for our children, we have done well by them. If we have not been a good model then it will show in our children. We may not like what we see, but our children are our mirrors. This is a hard truth but rewarding as well. Why? We can always turn and start making better decisions.

We have heard people say, and we have maybe said it ourselves, that we no longer know if we are a Christian because we don't want to do the right thing or admit to a sin. We know in our heart that God would not like what we are doing. We feel the guilt but don't want to face the truth or God about our sin. We are out of alignment with him. When this is the case we don't take into consideration how we throw our kids under the bus by rebelling against God. When we do this, we are acting as cowards, instead of realizing God wants to forgive us so we can have an intimate relationship with him and each other. We fear judgment from others and don't want to face our shame.

We make excuses even when we know the truth about spiritual consequences or behavioral psychology of recreating the behavioral patterns of our parents. We choose to hide behind a lie. We are scared and therefore lie, then pass this trait onto our children. It's heartbreaking to watch our children suffer then recreate the learned behavior. But these are our cycles. We need to be courageous enough to make the choice and say, "Enough!" and stop the cycle in our own generation. We stop our cycle by stopping the learned pattern that we know is wrong. We override the pattern by doing what we know is right in the eyes of God, our Daddy.

Our children mirror back our behavior. If we rage, they will rage. If we lie, they will lie. If we steal, they will steal. If we physically abuse our children, they will be violent and will physically abuse others. If we sexually abuse our children, chances are likely they will sexually abuse their children or others. If we disrespect our spouse, children learn it is okay to disrespect their spouse or allow disrespect toward themselves. We need to take a step toward stopping this behavior by healing the hurt within ourselves so these generational cycles stop, at least within our own generation. It's time for us as a family of Christians to step up and be accountable and stop being weak willed. We were made to be courageous, not cowards. One Christian contemporary band named, "Casting Crowns" sings of this very problem in a song entitled, "Courageous." They sing,

> "We could be the generation
> That finally breaks the chain"

The cycle continues unless we make a change. The cycle continues until we say, "Stop!" These generational cycles are curses which remain with us, and our children, until we allow the Holy Spirit to remove the sin within us, through our repentance. After our repentance, we must change our attitude and behavior from bitterness to love. This is a spiritual matter. If we cannot do this on our own, we need to ask a professional for help.

Making It Right

If we do not want our children to go through what we went through then we need to step up to the plate and hit a home run for ourselves and our future generations. We must make the changes necessary by making better choices for ourselves. It's not always easy but it is ever so rewarding in this realm and the one to come. It's bigger than us individually. We as individuals make the changes that ultimately change our generational cycles. We do not want our children picking up after us for what we have dumped on them.

We remember the laws of the Lord, by *doing* what we believe God is guiding our hearts to do. When we obey the guidance of the Holy Spirit, and what is written within the Scriptures, our children are not forgotten, but rather remembered, protected and blessed.

We are all guilty of making poor choices or looking the other way when we see others make poor choices. Because we are one body in Christ we have a responsibility to pray for each other and to confess our sins to each other so we can be a healthy body. The book of James says, "Therefore confess your sins to each other and pray for each other so that you may be healed. The prayer of a righteous person is powerful and effective" (James 5:16 NIV).

We are here on earth together. We need each other whether we want to admit it or not. We need to help each other and build each other up, not tear each other down. We may feel overwhelmed by thinking of the issues we need to repent of or feel we cannot make the huge change from our way of living to doing the right thing all of the time. But as we take one step at a time it becomes easier. We have all heard, "Rome wasn't built in a day." Well we are not going to be transformed in a day, but we can at least start walking in the right direction.

Second Corinthians 7:1 says, "Since we have these promises, dear friends, let us purify ourselves from everything that contaminates body and spirit, perfecting holiness out of reverence for God." As we begin to understand more clearly what the Bible has to tell us, we see God's promises are conditional. We will not receive all of his promises if we are not doing our part and putting some effort into our situation.

After we become born again believers, we are forgiven for our sins, and we are on our way to heaven when we die, or when Jesus returns. If we sin after our conversion we are out of fellowship with God and the one(s) we've sinned against. We are no longer in alignment with each other. So we need to ask for forgiveness to get back into having a more intimate relationship with God and others. If we make a mistake, then God is just, and he will forgive us of our mistake when we ask for forgiveness. It is good when we as Christians extend the same graciousness and forgive those who have sinned against us. This helps to keep the body of Christ in unity (Ephesians 4:3).

We are not perfect but we can at least acknowledge when we are wrong, and begin to make better choices. If we don't, there is a growing guilt within us. If this guilt is left unattended, it will grow like a cancer and we will manifest our guilt within our physical bodies. This could be a headache, stomachache, ulcer, or worse if left unattended. We may try to forget about our sin, but our body, soul, and heart will hold the memory, and it will be manifested. God wants us to purify ourselves so He can bless us. It's that simple. It's our choice.

God wants us to use our free will to make decisions which line up with his ways. When we are making decisions of righteousness, we are perfecting holiness within ourselves and the body of Christ. We are overriding our fleshly nature with the knowledge of God. We are choosing to rise above the natural situation and deal with it in a loving and faith-based way. This is our power against what we know is not right in our lives and it eventually becomes our new nature.

As Christians we have the opportunity, some would say responsibility, to cleanse ourselves from unrighteousness. Will this happen over night? No! Is it easy: Not always... We work at it every day, little by little; step by step.

We have both a moral and immoral part within us. Our moral part comes from God. The immoral part comes from unresolved sin in our lives which, when unattended could be used by our spiritual enemy to destroy us (John 10:10).

First Corinthians 3:16-17 says, "Don't you know that you yourselves are God's temple and that God's Spirit lives in you? If anyone destroys God's temple, God will destroy him; for God's temple is sacred, and you are that temple."

We collectively, as the body of Christ, are the temple of God. We are the church. We are not a building but our individual bodies have Christ dwelling within. This is powerful. We have buildings where we go and worship together as the body which is also powerful. But more importantly, we have a responsibility to protect ourselves as well as each other. We have the responsibility to not defile or dishonor anyone in any way.

When we choose to dishonor any part of our body, we may not understand the ramifications in the moment, but the consequences always come eventually. When we are acting negatively toward anyone in the body we are hurting ourselves, not just that person. We have all acted negatively toward someone within the body. We feel the pain in our heart when we do so. It is good to act quickly and ask for forgiveness. We are all learning as we mature in the ways of Christ. It's not always easy to keep asking for forgiveness. But we will continue to get stronger and more mature as we continue to do our best. Obviously it is important we learn this principle sooner rather than later.

So how in the world are we supposed to live here on earth? It is hard enough to walk down the street without judging someone or being judged. Galatians chapter 5 tells us we have freedom to choose right from wrong. It also states if we live by the Spirit of God we will not give in to the sinful nature. But let's face it, we have all given in at one time or another. It's not always easy.

Galatians 5:13 says it like this: "You, my brothers, were called to be free. But do not use your freedom to indulge the sinful nature; rather, serve one another in love." As we are serving one another in love we are not judging them. What does it mean by "serving them"? Well, how about if we just listen to them? That in itself is a start. Sometimes we just need someone to hear us, or give some thoughtful advice. Galatians 5:14 states, "The entire law is summed up in a single command: 'Love your neighbor as yourself.'" Is that not incredible!

The entire law in this new administration comes down to loving someone as you would love yourself. This is the golden rule. Do unto others as you would have others do unto you. These words are indeed gold. On the other hand, if we are mean spirited toward each other, we are destroyed by each other (Galatians 5:15). It apparently doesn't work very well when we are gossiping and back-biting each other.

It all comes down to Galatians 5:16-18: "So I say, live by the Spirit, and you will not gratify the desires of the sinful nature. For the sinful nature desires what is contrary to the Spirit, and the Spirit what is contrary to the sinful nature. They are in conflict with each other, so that you do not do what you want. But if you are led by the Spirit, you are not under law."

What does it mean to live by the Spirit of God? Or be led by the Spirit? It means when we know the correct thing to do in a situation, or believe the Spirit of God is guiding us and we follow his lead, we are protected. We are not under the law per se.' Just as Jesus healed a man on the Sabbath, we too are to follow the lead of the Spirit. There are many of us who believe in God but are weak willed when it comes to following either the Spirit, or avoiding temptations. However when we walk with the Spirit we are strengthened and temptations are easier to overcome.

The real question is what do we want? When we want what God wants for us we can go after it with every effort of our being! We have the power to choose right from wrong and God's ways are far better than what we can imagine for ourselves. We know this when we remember he created us and knows us better than we know ourselves. When we choose what God has placed in our pathway, it is ours if we play the game his way. It's not hard, it sometimes takes time and therefore patience, but we can enjoy what God has given to us. We can learn while on our journey. It is worth living our lives for and with the ones we truly love and who truly love us.

"For he chose us in him before the creation of the world to be holy and blameless in his sight. In love he predestined us to be adopted as his sons through Jesus Christ, in accordance with his pleasure and will" (Ephesians 1:4-5). God has plans for us and by now we should realize his ways are kingdom ways which far exceed our ways. He has predestinated us before the foundations of this world and it would behoove us to reach our destinations (Romans 8:30). This takes spiritual strength and courage. We ultimately change our destination in this life as we follow the move of the Holy Spirit in our lives.

We do not want to let our Heavenly Father, our creator, our Daddy down. For God's sake, he did not let us down. Jesus mediates for us every day. He knows we are made from dust and are weak, but we are also made in his image which overpowers any weakness. He has given us the tools to get his work done. Whether the tools are from the Holy Spirit or from the abilities we possess individually, they are tools with which he has enabled us to perform his plans. The choice is always ours.

Audio and E-books Playlist Chapter 3:

Sanctus Real—Whatever You Are Doing
http://www.youtube.com/watch?v=iN9J8eqKovY

Casting Crowns—Courage
http://www.youtube.com/watch?v=pkM-gDcmJeM

Mandisa—He Is With You
http://www.youtube.com/watch?v=F6hnmFbnGc4

Toby Mac—Lose My Soul
http://www.youtube.com/watch?v=coHKdhAZ9hU

Questions for chapter 3

1. Why is it important for you to have the courage to change?
2. How can you change your current situation?
3. Where do you see yourself one year from now? Five years from now?
4. What are the steps you must take in order to reach your destination?
5. Are your goals in alignment with what you know God wants for you?
6. Write an outline on how you want to approach your change calendar.

Doing Things God's Way

"The Lord will establish you as a holy people to Himself, just as He has sworn to you, if you keep the commandments of the Lord your God and walk in His ways. Then all peoples of the earth shall see that you are called by the name of the Lord, and they shall be afraid of you."

Deuteronomy 28:9-10

Do we know anyone who is afraid of us because we are known for being God's chosen people? Not many of us are known for such a thing. We are known for things like our intelligence, accomplishments, parenting skills or lack of them, or who we are in the community. We as Christians are far from holy these days. We lie, cheat, steal, have or want other things before God, and often we want what our neighbor has. We don't have to look very far beyond our own front yard to see this is true. We as God's people are a mess. We may say we love God but we, more commonly than not, like to call our own shots.

We all need to be healed from something in our lives because none of us are perfect or have arrived at being who we want to be by any means. We may have some of God's promises, but we also have problems. The reality is as we begin to obey God's guidance he will begin to establish us as his holy people. The question now is do we want to be known as God's chosen people? Again, not much has changed from Moses's time, or even Adam and Eve's time period, eight thousand years ago.

If we want to be known as God's holy people we must simply read his Word, the Holy Bible. Many ministries suggest we read the Bible through in one year. This is a good goal. We could even read it in two years. It doesn't matter as long as we are reading. Some people pick a book of the Bible to read in a month, or a psalm every day. Regardless as to the course or time, everyone is different and we must do what is right for us individually. At the same time, reading the Bible is paramount in order to know God, so we know his ways and have opportunity to be known as his chosen people.

Some people hesitate in reading the Bible because they don't know which version of the Bible to read. There are many versions of the Bible and some people say one version is more accurate than another. However, we all learn from each version in our own way. Regardless of which version we read, we must remember the original was written by holy men of God as they were moved by the Holy Spirit (2 Timothy 3:16, 2 Peter 1:21).

The original versions were written in Hebrew, Greek, and Aramaic, so they needed to be translated into English or other languages so we could read the Bible for ourselves. It was translated into Latin first and Martin Luther translated it into German because he believed the common people were intelligent enough to read and understand Scriptures for themselves. He saw the organized religion of that time period taking advantage of the common people and skewed the meaning for their own advantage. The organized religion of that day was obviously not too happy with Luther and that is one reason we now have the Lutheran church.

The King James Version of the Bible was translated for King James of England in 1611. That is why we see all of the "thee's" and "thou's" in that version. That is how they spoke. Newer translations like the New American Standard, Life Application and New International Versions are translations for our day and time so we can understand what we need to know in our culture, more clearly. Regardless of which version we read, they are all good and we can learn from all of them. In terms of being the most accurate to the original, some believe the New American Standard is closest and that is why it does not flow as nicely as other versions. Regardless to whichever version we choose, they all have purpose or they would not have been published. Regardless of which version we read, as we read we will be learning how to do things God's way which is the main point here. At the same time, by comparing versions, we can learn from each one and pull it all together as we ponder a passage or thought.

For instance, King James translates "obedience" to God as "hearkening" to God's voice. What does 'hearkening unto God's voice' mean? Webster says, it means to give responsive attention to something of importance. It means to hear intelligently, to diligently obey, and perhaps tell others. Hearkening sounds a little more intense than obedience possibly because of our over use of the word "obedience" in our culture.

As we hearken unto God's voice, (Holy Bible, Holy Spirit), not only are we glorifying God, but we are also receiving his favor. This means he protects and blesses us because of our obedience to him. This is how we get our internal peace. This is where we find comfort, security, and love for ourselves and each other. It is most difficult to love others if we do not love ourselves. We may love others in a fleeting moment, but our personality eventually comes out.

When we have an intimate relationship with God we love because he loves us. We cannot get away from it. It is automatic when we see the good in others because our relationship with God is real and we see the good in ourselves. We feel loved by God. It supersedes love from a human. Yet we still need to feel loved by humans. That is why God made Eve for Adam. He needed someone to love (Genesis 2:18-25).

Because we love and trust God, we choose to listen to him and do what he asks us to do for him. As we continue to hearken unto God's voice we are rising above our earthly situations because he is guiding us spiritually in the path in which he wants us to take with him. It becomes easier the more we are obedient to his ways. In fact, we no longer think of it as being obedient. We think of it as God asking us to do something for him, similarly to our parent asking us to do something for them.

Some people may call our obediencethe right or correct direction. Regardless of what we may call it, it is God's direction to follow if we want to be known as his kids, or his chosen people. As we continue to follow his guidance, our trust in the LORD becomes stronger along with greater discernment of right and wrong. This is not a hard thing to do as some may think. Nor is it rocket science. This is the kingdom of God working in us.

God's voice is the Holy Bible, Jesus Christ, and the Holy Spirit. Deuteronomy chapter 28 gives us practical knowledge of what was and what was not acceptable in Gods eyes for the Israelites. We can learn a lot from this chapter because we see the heart of God for his people. The first fourteen verses tell us God's promises are to those who love him, and therefore keep his commandments.

Deuteronomy 28:1-2 says, "Now it shall come to pass, if you diligently obey the voice of the Lord your God, to observe carefully all His commandments which I command you today, that the LORD your God will set you high above all nations of the earth. And all these blessings shall come upon you and overtake you, because you obey the voice of the LORD your God:"

Although we may be under a new administration of the law of love and the move of the Holy Spirit, we still need to realize the Ten Commandments remain true for us today. The reason for knowing these laws is the same reason as it was three thousand and two hundred years ago when Moses wrote them. We need them because we are in need of direction. They are the voice of the LORD. Sometimes we need to be reminded because our will is sometimes weak. We may have the Holy Spirit working through us but we still have free choice and knowing what God's will is helps us make wise choices which protect us and our future. Obedience to God is written throughout the Bible. We can find reason after reason to obey. The choice is ultimately ours.

The point here is if we, as a literal nation, diligently obeyed the voice of the Lord and observed his commandments we, as a nation, would be high above all other nations, just as the Israelites were when they obeyed the voice of the Lord. This is true for any nation. This is true for the body of Christ. This is a collective promise in that we 'as a nation' or as the body of Christ as a nation, must act as one in unity. With all of the different faiths throughout the world today, this is a hard requirement, however even one person can make an impact as did Daniel.

The Strength of Daniel

As we consider Israel and how strong they were in the beginning, but later turned away from God and his ways, we see the rather unseemly consequences. God delivered them out of Egypt. He got them through the desert. Joshua led them into victory as they entered into the 'promised land.' They had prophets to guide them and even kings who were not always faithful. Eventually they 'bowed down to other gods' in that they got caught up in the world around them. This is an on-going theme throughout our history.

We, just as the Israelites, get side tracked by the eye candy around us. We see how Israel looked around and saw other ways of doing things from the other peoples in the lands in which they took over. They later defiled the temple with offerings that were tainted, stolen, crippled and sick (Malachi chapter 1). They were not giving God their best as in Cain's situation. They were giving an offering they did not want for themselves. They were giving an offering they would not offer a human king in that day. They no longer reverenced God with their best.

They were eventually taken over by the Babylonian's because of their arrogant, selfish, and disobedient behavior. They were put into exile for seventy years, but God rescued them and used the ones who loved and respected him, Daniel, Meshach, Shadrach, and Abed-Nego. God used those who trusted in him to show his continued love and promises to his people. He has not changed. God still uses us, his kids who trust and therefore obey him. He uses us when we are hesitant. He uses us even when we feel we have no choice in the matter. He uses us because he has chosen us to do a job for him. It's up to us whether we say yes or no.

Daniel was one of the many exiles carried away to Babylon. He was around sixteen-years-old and yet was known to have an 'excellent spirit' in him among this polytheistic nation. He was highly ranked among the Babylonian leaders to be an advisor to their kings. He practiced the laws of God, and he prayed three times a day because he loved his relationship with God. He knew the importance of keeping God's laws and he observed firsthand the consequences of disobedience to the earthly king. Daniel desired an intimate relationship with God. He knew God was the only one who could get him through the mess in which his ancestors had put him and the rest of Israel.

Because other leaders were jealous of Daniel they tricked King Darius into changing a law which would not allow Daniel's kind of prayer. When the law of the land changed and Daniel knew he would be thrown into the lions' den for praying to God, he stood firm in not changing his *practice* of prayer to the Most High for anyone. Daniel still respected and honored King Darius, but he also knew the significance of and the power of prayer.

When we look at Daniel's prayer life as a model in the midst of adversity, we see God's deliverance of him because of their relationship. God protected Daniel by sending his angel to shut the mouths of lions (Daniel 6). Because of Daniel's desire for intimacy with, and faithfulness to God, God trusted him. God later gave Daniel one of the greatest Biblical revelations. Parts of this revelation correspond with the book of Revelation the Apostle John wrote six hundred years later.

The Power of Prayer and Obedience

Prayer and obedience to God is far greater than sacrificing our relationship with him. It is our love for him, along with our faith and hope in him that are the main ingredients to our relationship with him. These five ingredients (love, prayer, obedience, faith, hope) are the foreshadowing of the Holy Spirit working in us, enabling the kingdom of God's expression to flow through us more frequently.

As we carefully observe God's commandments, we know the right thing to do in any given situation. This is the righteousness James 5:16 speaks of, "...confess your sins to each other and pray for each other so that you may be healed. The prayer of a righteous person is powerful and effective."

As we do what is right, we are righteous in God's sight. When we are hearkening unto God, he gives us the desires of our heart because of our relationship with him. When we get our heart and ways aligned with God's heart and ways, we are acting as his kids. Our prayers will be honored because we believe, and we don't ask for anything unrealistic.

On the other hand, when we are not in alignment with God, He does not have to honor our prayers because that is not his promise to us. Sometimes our prayers are all over the place because we are confused or lost in our own ways. Sometimes we just want what we want, when we want it, not necessarily wanting what is in line with God. So we don't always get what we ask for. We pout. We rage. We have a temper tantrum and screw up again because we don't get our way. We are spoiled, especially in America. We have had so many things handed to us we don't know how or want to work for them. When we are asked to work, we complain. Why? We have not been disciplined.

Sometimes God surprises us and gives us what we have asked for before we expect it. We may think something needs to happen first in our lives before God will bless us with what we have asked. But we are not the ones in control. He is. When our prayers are answered in a way we don't understand, we just thank him! God loves us and perhaps he believes in us more than we believe in ourselves. By us asking him for anything, we are returning to him by our simple request in our prayers. Acknowledgment of him at any level shows him we do believe. God's timing may not always be what we expect, it is however accurate and perfect. That is the part we need to trust. But we don't always.

When we don't get what we have asked for we might throw a fit and walk away from God altogether. We have all had our temper tantrums with each other and with God. This shows our maturity level, or lack of it. We might even try to get everyone on our side to feel sorry for us and try to convince people that God doesn't *really* want anything good for us. This might sound a little harsh but we have all seen this happen or we may have played the 'feel sorry for me' game ourselves.

If we think about it, this is exactly what Lucifer did before he fell from grace. Because of pride in his heart, he simply did not want to adhere to God's ways and his ultimate authority. Lucifer wanted to be the authority. So, just like in Lucifer's case, behind our rebellion is pride, and "pride goes before destruction, a haughty spirit before a fall" (Proverbs 16:18). What does it mean to have a haughty spirit? It is the same thing as having an arrogant or cavalier attitude. It's not good. God wins this one and he always will. We are the ones who need to check our attitude at the door when it comes to God. We might be able to get away with this attitude with other people, but let's face it, God is bigger. He may love us but he is not going to let us manipulate him or take advantage of his kids. He will avenge those he loves and who are faithful to him. Romans 12:19 says it this way, "Do not take revenge, my friends, but leave room for God's wrath, for it is written: 'It is mine to avenge; I will repay,' says the Lord."

Again, as we are obedient to God's voice and ways, he will listen and act upon our prayer requests because of our relationship with him. Why? Because through our loving obedience we show our love, respect, and trust in him.

If we want a relationship with our creator who wants us to call him "Daddy," as Jesus did, we need to understand his commandments, carefully observe them by doing them with our respectful and loving heart. We will receive blessings earned by our obedience, and we are being good examples for our children. Our children will learn from our obedience and our disobedience. As we give them Godly wisdom and guidance by words or example, we are providing good soil for our own seeds to grow and prosper. More importantly, we are delighting in our own relationship with our creator, who wants to be our Dad, who wants to bless us, who wants us to enjoy the kingdom of God here on earth while we are here now. We don't have to wait for anything! Our obedience is our down payment for prayers requested.

Audio and E-Books Play List Chapter 4:

Switchfoot—Restless
http://www.youtube.com/watch?v=GiiQcyoKWjQ

Jeremy Camp—Let It Fade
http://www.youtube.com/watch?v=h843f2GXie0

Josh Wilson—Before the Morning
http://www.youtube.com/watch?v=0JYGhQWgqq4

Superchick—We Live
http://www.youtube.com/watch?v=C_whi9GmAO8

Questions for Chapter 4

1. Do you want to be known as one of "God's chosen people"?
2. Are you able to hearken unto the Lord's voice?
3. Do you feel the move of the Holy Spirit in your life?
4. Ask God what you can do to please Him today.

Taking Responsibility

"Those who conceal their sins do not prosper, but those who confess and renounce them find mercy."

Proverbs 28:13

"Like a city whose walls are broken down is a man who lacks self-control."

Proverbs 26:28

Taking responsibility for our feelings of pain or even our short comings is not always easy because let's face it, life is not always easy. In fact, sometimes life is down-right hard and disappointing. The funny thing about life is we wouldn't exchange life for not having been born.

We have heard it said: "Life is not fair." The Bible says all God's ways are just (Deuteronomy 32:4). Life is what we make of it, not necessarily what someone else has made it to be for us. In some of our cases it has been made to be hell and we need to figure a way to get out of our situation. Then we remember some people have it worse than us. When we consider human trafficking issues in America and around the world we know that is far worse than our situation.

We all have had our disappointments, heartaches and plenty of them. People disappoint us; we disappoint ourselves. We sabotage ourselves. Some disappointments are so excruciatingly painful we want to die because we cannot fathom what just happened. We relate to music on the radio from our favorite artists. We talk with friends and family. We cry. We grieve our loss.

We eventually either work it out by dealing with our internal feelings or we re-create the same disappointments. When we don't deal with our feelings, especially those from our past we bring issues onto ourselves unknowingly. We have feelings about what we are lacking within our personal lives. If not dealt with, these feelings then are transferred feelings and projections onto others. However, when we take responsibility for our feelings of pain, and work through our personal issues we have a greater understanding of who we are and why we have created our situations. It is very similar to generational cycles, but these we often create on our own.

Dealing with our problems then is a good thing for us. Many people do not want to go to counselors, but if we can find one who helps us work through our past issues, it's worth our time, effort, and money. We have to remember we are human and for some unknown reason, we get hurt. We live in a world with hurt people. Hurt people hurt others unless they are able to move through the pain and rise above their current situation. We as a human race are seemingly always peeling off layers of our emotional and spiritual baggage. We all have a need to fit in or belong. If this need is not met we again redefine who we are and what we want. Life is an on-going journey. If we would not change it for not being born, what do we do?

CHOICES

We as a human race have choices to make on a daily basis. Those choices are factored into our future and the future of those closest to us, our kids. Sometimes we worry about our situation or the decisions we have made. Sometimes we have a hard time trusting what someone has said to us. There is always something to consider.

One serenity statement reads: "The future belongs to those who believe in the beauty of their dreams." Sometimes that is where we need to start, with our dreams.

Matthew 6:31–34 says, "So do not worry, saying, 'What shall we eat?' or 'What shall we drink?' or 'What shall we wear?' For the pagans run after all these things, and your heavenly Father knows that you need them. But seek first his kingdom and his righteousness, and all these things will be given to you as well. Therefore do not worry about tomorrow, for tomorrow will worry about itself. Each day has enough trouble of its own."

This Scripture is profound, but sometimes the only part we can see is the "each day has enough trouble of its own." It may not be because we are not taking responsibility and pulling our own weight. There are other people in our lives who won't take responsibility for themselves or their actions. We are forced to deal with their irresponsibility. We may have been hurt by their words and behavior and yet they won't admit any wrongdoing. They lie and at some point we need to draw the line in the sand and realize there is nothing we can do for them. As we accept the situation for what it is, we pray and let them go; and, we move on.

On the other hand, we may be the ones who are not being responsible. Being honest and taking responsibility helps us stay focused on what is in front of us now. The future will take care of itself as we admit what we have said or done. Truth brings us peace. We then begin to see our future play out more beautifully. This behavioral style becomes easier as we practice. Courage is like a muscle. The more we use it the stronger it becomes. It takes courage to speak the truth when we have been wrong.

Taking responsibility is not always easy. If we did not grow up learning how to take responsibility for our actions it is harder for us to learn as adults. So, it would behoove us to teach responsibility to our children as one of the first things they learn. This is problematic if both parents are not in agreement which is common especially because of divorces. The kids suffer and have to learn for themselves. This is all part of our domino effect in generational cycles.

When we lack responsibility in our lives, apathy grows in our hearts for the things most important to us. In this particular case some hope is found in pre-marital counseling. It is helpful in discussing these types of issues before marriage. If we don't seek pre-marital counseling we end up reading books like this one. Or we seek professional help from someone who can shed some light on our situation. It's not a bad thing, but it is the case when we are at a loss as to what to do.

At least we search. We search because we want to love and don't want to be alone. We search because we all need help and at some point we are willing to admit it, at least when things get so bad we have to leave or get help.

Responsibility is all part of this ongoing process of being honest and living in harmony with one another. As believers we understand the importance of taking responsibility for everything we do and say because like it or not, the world and people around us are watching, just as we are watching others.

More importantly however, when we do not take responsibility for our actions, we may be allowing someone else to take the fall for us. Or if we are not telling the truth about something, we are asking someone to believe our lie. As previously mentioned this is manipulative and cowardly on our part and is driven by fear. This is confusing for the person we are not being honest with because internally they feel the lie. The disrespect of not speaking the truth defiles the relationship and tears it apart internally. It is felt by all parties whether spoken or not. This is emotionally abusive.

When we are not being honest and taking responsibility, we are not respecting God and clearly we are disrespecting those in whom we lie to. Knowingly or unknowingly, we are choosing to rebel against God and his ways. Just like when someone hurts one of our kids, we hurt; when we hurt one of God's kids, we hurt

God. When we hurt one of his kids he does not take too kindly to the pain his kids suffer. That is why there are consequences. Sooner or later he takes care of his own, just as we take care of our own. This is a good place to "be as shrewd as snakes and as innocent as doves" (Matthew 10:16).

When we think we cannot take responsibility it typically is because of our fear stemming from insecurities, a selfish nature, or a false belief. Often we learn as kids we are not allowed to use our voice. Meaning we feel we cannot speak up or we will be raged on, corrected, or shamed. Our voice may have been silenced by an abusive or controlling parent or guardian. The suppression of our voice suppresses us as a human being which often leads to feelings of shame. This shame can override emotions in regard to our own sense of self. We lack confidence.

To avoid feelings of shame we may make compensations and deny feelings altogether. We may hide ourselves by hiding our feelings. If our favorite color is red, we may say it is blue, just so we are not seen. Doing anything to not be known may be our goal. Misrepresenting ourselves eventually becomes a burden and shame is felt. At some point we hardly recognize our true feelings. No one knows us because we refuse to be known. But at some point we need to believe in ourselves enough to break out of our shell. Do and say what we believe. If we don't we are another tragic statistic.

This is one of the main reasons it is advantageous for us to read and/or study the Bible for ourselves. It gives us courage to say and do what we believe. It's good to go to church and Bible studies but God wants to know us individually and wants to see our interest in getting to know him. It is a courtship. When we allow conviction of our thoughts and heart, truth is revealed to us. We find opportunity to make better decisions. We find mercy after mercy as we continue to do what we know is right and true for us. And then, life throws us another curve ball to either peel off another emotional layer or God gives us a job we don't really want to do.

Jonah's Story

Jonah was given a job by God that he didn't want to do. As a prophet, Jonah had a responsibility to deliver God's message to the people of Nineveh. Because of Jonah's disgust and fear of the Ninevites, he chose to go as far away from Neneveh as possible. In fact Jonah went the opposite direction. He boarded a boat, went down in the bow of the boat, and fell asleep. A ferocious storm came. He admitted to the sailors the storm was because he disobeyed God.

The sailors reluctantly threw him overboard. The storm immediately stopped, and Jonah found himself in the belly of a whale. It was only when Jonah repented inside the whale that the whale regurgitated him out onto dry land.

We may not ever be in the belly of a whale, but we may be in a problematic situation which makes us feel as though we are encased with overwhelming phlegm, or emotions not coming from God. Confusion, fear, anger, shame, and guilt are many emotional 'red flags.'

At the same time, like Jonah, we may very well know why we are in our situation. We may know exactly what put us here and why things are no longer black and white. They are in the gray area and we just may need a revelation on how to get out of this one. So reading our Bible is good, but knowing what to do and choosing not to do it doesn't help us, just as in Jonah's case.

It's good to be responsible and do our part. It takes maybe five minutes to read a Scripture passage in the morning or at work. As we read for ourselves, we are guided. When we take responsibility in staying in step with the Spirit of God, we follow his lead. We may have trouble with this one starting out because it may not have been modeled for us or made routine. The more we follow his lead though, the easier and more adventurous our journey becomes. Reading our Bible is a lifestyle that gives us courage and strength for our day to day walk no matter who we are or what we do.

Going Back to the Basics

Another way to help us with responsibility is to go back to the basics. Going back to the basics leads us to the book of Genesis. Genesis gives us insights on the first of many behaviors and attitudes recorded. We see similarities in what works, and what does not work in our own lives.

Some people joke about Adam and Eve, and wonder how they could have committed the first sin. Yet we need to remember God created them first, and they therefore were extremely intelligent. They had daily, intimate conversations with God without the intrusion of defiant thoughts. They were in step with the Spirit of God.

There were no generational curses or cycles inherited when they were created. Therefore, there was no injustice in their hearts. Eventually they chose to defy God, and now injustice lives in everyone's heart. That is what we fight against every day in our hearts and minds. If we don't overtake these thoughts of injustice toward God and others, it will not take long for them to grow into the same extent as Cain killing his own brother Abel. Some may think this to be extreme but if we look around, we see it happening on a daily basis. No one is exempt from taking responsibility for their own actions. It eats away at us because it's un-dealt with sin which creates guilt in our hearts. When we don't deal with our issues we are fighting an internal battle within ourselves. We project our pain and confusion onto others just like Cain did with Abel.

As we look at this logically we see how God gave Cain an out. But Cain wanted to do things his way. Kind of like us. God always gives us a way out of our temptations as well. It is up to us to take responsibility for our situation and rule over the temptation or injustice in our heart.

It all started with Cain and Abel giving an offering to God. Abel's offering was acceptable to God but Cain's was not. Genesis 4:5-8 explains Cain's situation like this, "… but on Cain and his offering He (God) did not look with favor. So Cain was very angry, and his face was downcast. Then the LORD said to Cain, 'Why are you angry? Why is your face downcast? If you do what is right, will you not be accepted? But if you do not do what is right, sin is crouching at your door, it desires to have you, but you must rule over it.' Now Cain said to his brother Abel, 'Let's go out to the field. While they were in the field, Cain attacked his brother Abel and killed him."

We are always given ways out of doing something wrong. This entire situation stemmed from Cain giving God an unacceptable offering. His brother Abel gave an acceptable offering. Cain was angry at God for not accepting him or his offering, and he was jealous of Abel because he did the right thing in God's eyes, and therefore was accepted by God.

We do this sometimes. We get jealous because someone is given an award over us or is congratulated for doing a good job. Or we get upset with a kid because they won an award over our own kid. We are the one with the problem. If we do what is right we will be accepted. We may not get an award but we feel accepted in God's eyes. Is that not most important?

Cain would have been accepted if he had given God an acceptable offering. God even gave Cain a second chance to give an acceptable offering. This could have been the end of the story. He may have known what an acceptable offering was, if not, he could have asked. Yet God knew Cain's heart. He was cheating or slighting the offering and God wasn't going to sugar coat it and accept it anyway.

Cain could have done what he knew was right. But he did not. Then we have our first murder. When Cain was told by God sin was crouching at his door and desired to have him for lunch, Cain did what he wanted to do anyway. He kept back part of the offering, thereby not giving God what he knew was right and his jealousy grew for Abel. That sin of jealousy overtook Cain and he killed his brother Abel. How often do we see killings in the news over jealousy? We must rule over it and all other emotions that are not from God.

When we consider doing what we know is wrong, sin lies at our door. It desires us. We are the ones who need to *rule* over it by being honest and dealing with it directly and immediately. We can do what Cain did and not ask God, "What is acceptable?"

By going back a little further in Genesis, we see Adam and Eve also knew full well not to eat of the Tree of Knowledge of Good and Evil. Together, they had a huge garden to attend to and both of them had dominion over all the animals. They probably grew to love and respect each other and the animals very much.

If we think about this for a moment, Satan could have been scheming for quite a while before he first deceived Eve. He could have been watching for any weakness between the two of them, just as he watches for weaknesses in us, especially in our marriages. He found the weakness. Then only through charm, deception, and manipulation Satan tricked Eve. Neither he, nor his method, has changed. A lot of women are taken advantage of in this same way today.

Satan is the Father of lies. So if we have an issue with lying we know where it stems from. If our problem or addiction is ruining our lives, or the lives of others, we can do as those in Alcoholics Anonymous do and, 1) take it one day at a time, 2) tell a trusted friend and, 3) be accountable. In other words, be responsible for our behavior. We all need help when faced with troubles and temptations. We may think we can handle it alone, but that is a false belief and a lie we cannot afford to fight on our own. We need each other in good times and in bad. We are a body fitly joined together.

Adam and Eve wanted to obey the voice of the Lord because they loved and respected their creator. They had a daily routine of communicating in the 'cool of the day.' Satan knew if he could get Eve to eat the forbidden fruit he would have divided the two. She would eventually have to talk with Adam about her sin and this may cause separation. Or Adam would choose to sin as well and join his wife. This manipulating scheme continues to be one of his biggest strategies today in marriages.

Simply put, when we are not taking responsibility for our wrongful actions toward others, we choose to rebel against God's ways. We become like Adam and Eve when they rebelled against God, and ate from the Tree of Knowledge of Good and Evil. They did not murder like Cain, nor did they commit adultery like King David. They simply did not obey God's command of "do not eat from the Tree of Knowledge of Good and Evil." They rebelled against God by doing what he specifically told them not to do.

Their entire world was turned upside down because they now had iniquity living in their hearts and thereby, sinful thoughts being brought to their minds. They lost their undisturbed intimate relationship with God, and they were kicked out of the Garden of Eden.

After they ate from the tree there is no record stating they repented, but rather that they hid themselves from God and made excuses. They did not take responsibility. When we sin, we also try to hide or deny our sin. Why do we hide? Because we are afraid, just as Adam and Eve were afraid. They were afraid because they were ashamed of their sin. They were ashamed of their nakedness whereas before, they were not.

They knew they did the one thing God asked them not to do. When we sin (and don't take responsibility) we live in denial, and our heart condemns us. Our heart becomes hardened and we become bitter. This is when our own bitterness gets misplaced and projected onto other people. We blame others, we make excuses, we are bitter. This is where we move away from God, others, our self, and our original purpose. Just like Adam and Eve.

In brief, what happened next with Adam and Eve and the generations that followed were a series of sins. The continuation of sin goes on today because iniquity was birthed in their hearts when they ate from the tree of knowledge of good and evil. What is iniquity? Iniquity is sin, evil, injustice, unfairness or wickedness to name a few.

After Adam ate from the tree he did not take responsibility for his choice. He said to God, "The woman You put here with me—she gave me some fruit from the tree, and I ate it." Eve said, "The serpent deceived me, and I ate" (Genesis 3:12-13). Nothing has changed. We still find it difficult to say, "I chose to do what I knew was wrong. I'm sorry."

Adam trusted the woman, possibly because he saw that she was not 'surely dead' physically, and Eve trusted the serpent. They did not check it out with God first and there is no record of repentance. Maybe they thought it was too late to repent because the damage was done. Maybe they didn't know how to repent. We don't know.

The point is they did not take responsibility. They blamed others for their sin. Adam blamed Eve and God. Eve blamed the serpent. Just as we sometimes blame God and others for our failures and choices to sin.

We don't know if they knew how to take responsibility because they had never sinned before or if this was their new way of thinking because not only did sin enter their lives, they just ate from the tree of knowledge of good and evil. Prior to this, they only knew what was good. Now they also knew what was evil. They were tricked! Because they were tricked, we now get tricked. Now that is not fair! But God's ways are just... Once the original sin was committed, iniquity was born in their hearts. It continues now through us and is passed on to future generations. Rebellion continues to work through us today when we choose to do what we know is wrong. The battle begins in our minds and then is played out by our actions.

Thank God for Jesus because we at least have an advocate who fights for us and the Holy Spirit who guides us. If we follow them we can manifest the Kingdom of God here on Earth. But it certainly is not always easy. Pain is often involved because of our fallen world and our generations of struggling. But we are overcoming with the blood of the lamb (Jesus Christ) and the words of our mouth (Revelation 12:11).

James 1:14 states, "each of you is tempted when you are dragged away by your own evil desire and enticed." This Scripture tells us what is behind our temptation, our own evil desire. This possibly means then at some point Eve and Adam may have been curious, and eventually desired to eat from the tree of knowledge of good and evil. They knew what God said, but at some point, they wanted more. Perhaps they lost sight of what they had, and were no longer content because they were tempted to doubt God and therefore, they rebelled against him. Does any of this sound familiar?

This is an incredible realization in that we may no longer want to sin in a particular area of our life. Yet because sin was birthed in our ancestors, it is sometimes very difficult to let it go. If it is generational, then it is called a generational cycle or curse. These terms are intermixed. This is why we may need to ask for help. Ultimately, if God says we can rule over sin, then we can rule over sin—any sin. It is our choice. We can rule over sin even if it is a stronghold.

Breaking the Cycles and Moving Forward

Thank God for Jesus Christ, the Holy Spirit, and the Holy Scriptures which help us kill off the strongholds and this sinful nature. We sometimes need good council as well. Formational Prayer, or Spiritual Formation is up and coming in terms of being known for its powerful impact on overcoming generational cycles, strongholds, and healing the brokenness within ones heart. Healing Care Ministries founded by Dr. Terry Wardle of Ashland Theological Seminary is the founder of this type of counsel. It is one of the best healing models of this nature.

Too often we think we can handle something on our own. If we can, then that is great! If we can't then we are wrong. This is when we need good, strong, professional help along with a strong support system. When we have good counsel along with loving support we will not only fight these battles together, but overcome them and rule over temptation. If we have either intimacy or abandonment issues we too often become loners because we feel we cannot trust anyone. But we all need a good support system. And it's okay to ask for help.

As we choose to take responsibility for our own weaknesses by praying to God for strength and understanding, then choose to do what we know is right, we are killing our sinful nature with the righteousness of God. This is a process of purification within our hearts and souls. Our nature eventually becomes God's nature as we continue to follow him. This process is a gradual one. Yet it is worth our every effort and every righteous decision!

As mentioned in chapter one it takes approximately thirty days for a new habit to begin forming. It takes about three months to build upon that habit creating our new character. Studies show depending on the habit we want to change the average for a successful change is sixty-six days. (Phillippa Lally, University College London, *European Journal of Social Psychology*.) It is recommended to receive support during these times of change whether from friends or professional counselors. We know our own strengths and weaknesses. Therefore it is important we get the help we need.

As we read the Bible it purifies our thoughts and equips us with understanding. It thereby counteracts against the evil thoughts we receive due to the eating from the tree of knowledge of good and evil. As we build our understanding of Biblical history it is not only informative it is wisdom learned from our creator. As we meditate on the Word of God we have greater discernment and therefore make better decisions. As we make changes in our lives which reflect our creator, we are transforming our lives into the life in which God intends for us to have. We are transforming our lives to that of a child of God and therefore we reap the rewards. This does not mean we will not have problems. We will always have problems. It is our character that decides how we will handle the problems.

We will always have temptations coming into our mind because of the original sin, and we need to be on guard for ourselves and our family. One way to keep our minds and hearts guarded is to simply read and meditate on the Scriptures daily. This is an easy first step and cannot be emphasized enough! In fact our enemy does not want us to think about reading the Bible because he fears we will be strengthened spiritually and make better decisions so he cannot control us or our families as much. He is correct.

First Corinthians 14:33a tells us, "God is not the author of confusion but of peace." The book of 2 Corinthians, chapter ten, tells us our warfare is in our thoughts. "The weapons we fight with are not the weapons of the world. On the contrary, they have divine power to demolish strongholds. We demolish arguments and every pretension that sets itself up against the knowledge of God, and we take captive every thought to make it obedient to Christ" (2 Corinthians 10:4-5).

Just as the Apostle Paul spoke to the Corinthians, we as Christians have the capability, and some would say, responsibility, to take our thoughts into captivity. We often want to entertain ungodly thoughts because we are human. However, in order to overcome strongholds we must bring them under our control and not entertain them. This is easier when we are around like-minded believers. We find it more difficult to do when hanging around people who don't care about God or his ways. However, we can control the thoughts if we put our mind to it. Or, we can choose to leave our surroundings.

As Christians, we have a responsibility to keep ourselves and our thoughts from evil. We make choices that will either keep us out of trouble, or create trouble for us. This is how Eve was deceived. She began talking with the serpent, entertaining thoughts of rebellion and unrighteousness. We could learn from her behavior.

When we do not do what we know is right in God's eyes, we open the door to our own fate. We lose our sovereign protection from God through our choice to disobey his righteous ways. This is because when we blatantly choose to do what we know is wrong, we open the door to the kingdom of this world. By our sin, that kingdom now has a 'spiritual right' to come into our lives and steal, kill or destroy us and our family.

We can stop wondering why bad things keep happening to us. We have been part of the problem and may not have known it. But, now we do know. If we aren't taking steps to help heal ourselves spiritually, we need to stop crying out "poor me!" When we begin taking responsibility we will begin to see changes for the good in our lives.

As we continue our journey with God by obeying his voice and his ways, we begin to feel his peace that passes all understanding. It is not hard to be nice to someone or even to tell the truth about something. Somehow life seems easier because we are being more honest and more Christ-like in our thoughts, words and actions.

It is time for the body of Christ to take control of our lives by controlling thoughts and choices. This is an opportunity for us to see God work in our favor. This is love for our self, our family, and our Heavenly Father. This is having integrity, and being responsible for who God has created us to be. This is an opportunity to allow the kingdom of God to manifest through us, and our obedience.

Audio and E-Books Play List Chapter 5:

Article One—I'm Not Alright
http://www.youtube.com/watch?v=FAJnK4zgWpo

Third Day—Revelation
http://www.youtube.com/watch?v=IOfoXDymFZA

MercyMe—Hurt and the Healer
http://www.youtube.com/watch?v=M19k7a0DvAc

Francesca Battistelli—Beautiful
http://www.youtube.com/watch?v=JbCfyZHSQbE

QUESTIONS FOR CHAPTER 5

1. What do you need to take responsibility for in your life right now?
2. What is your first step?
3. Make a plan to see it through.
4. Work the plan.

Our Battle ... Our Victory

"Yet a time is coming and has now come when the true worshipers will worship the Father in spirit and truth."

John 4:23

"But the Counselor, the Holy Spirit, whom the Father will send in my name, will teach you all things and will remind you of everything I have said to you."

John 14:26

"You are of God, little children, and have overcome them, because He who is in you is greater than he who is in the world."

I John 4:4

These three Scripture passages refer to three separate but intertwining revelations.

1. True worshippers worship God in spirit and in truth.
2. The Holy Spirit is our Counselor and tells us things we need to know.
3. There is dynamite power inside of us that can demolish what is in this world.

Why do we need to know we are capable of overpowering something in the world? Why do we need a spiritual Counselor? Why do we need to worship God in spirit and in truth? The answer to all of these questions is simple. Although we live in a physical body and world it includes a spiritual battle behind the scenes.

We are more than just bodies and minds. We are spiritual beings within our bodies. We each have our own mind and soul where we think and feel love, pain, and everything in between. We also have access to our Heavenly Father through the Holy Spirit and Christ Jesus. The Holy Spirit is constantly counseling us, yet we are not always accepting of his counsel. He is a gentleman. He will not overpower us. We always have a choice to listen and obey his words of advice.

Jesus is the Christ. We too have Christ in us which is our dynamite power which overtakes what is coming at us in this world. How do we know what is coming at us? That is where the Holy Spirit comes to our minds and speaks to us. In a way, we have this sixth sense. He counsels our mind and we sense the truth in our soul. We know what is going on without a person telling us because we sense the Spirit of God telling us. There are some cases where the Holy Spirit may tell many people the same thing. When this is the case it is his way of giving confirmation of his move in a matter.

Second Corinthians 10:4-6 tells us,

> The weapons we fight with are not the weapons of the world. On the contrary, they have divine power to demolish strongholds. We demolish

> arguments and every pretension that sets itself up against the knowledge of God, and we take captive every thought to make it obedient to Christ. And we will be ready to punish every act of disobedience, once your obedience is complete.

So what is this telling us? The battle is in our mind, with every thought. We compare our thoughts with those of Christ and what we know from the Bible. Hence, a good reason to know what is in it. When we know the truth about the Scriptures, we speak them into being. When we are in right standing with God we make our way through trials by our attitude and the words of truth we speak.

The weapons we fight with are our faith based words. Our words have authority because the Spirit of God is working through us. Therefore, our words have divine power to demolish the strongholds and arguments coming against us and trying to tear down our ideas, projects, books, music, or whatever we are working on. When we take into consideration every thought and compare it to the righteousness of God, we speak either for or against that thought.

To help our understanding and in order to have the confidence we are hearing from the Holy Spirit, it is helpful to be in a good relationship with our Heavenly Father at the time. This is not new, but rather a reminder of the importance of our ongoing relationship with the Father. We waver because we are not perfect, but we know how to get back into alignment with him.

Additionally, in order to increase our odds of receiving what we ask for, it is best to have that good relationship with our Father. We know to do this by obeying his commands and doing what pleases him (1 John 3:21-22).

This is not new and may appear redundant and/or esoteric to many. But if we are honest, we can all say we sense the Spirit of God in our lives. If we say we don't, as Christians we are in denial. We are connected to God so there is no way we cannot feel his movement in our lives. It is we who decide to allow him to move freely in our lives or not because of our free will.

We need to act like Jesus which is possible because Philippians 2:5 says, "Let this mind be in you that was also in Christ." And 1 Corinthians 2:16 says, "… we have the mind of Christ." Plus, when we are in need of a refresher because let's face it, we all get stressed out in this world, we have the capability of renewing our mind in the spirit (Ephesians 4:23).

When we have a good relationship with God, all things are possible. When God asked Jesus to do something, he did it, even when it was unconventional. This is how we are to behave as well. This life as a Christian is a journey. It may not be what we thought, because we never know where the road of life in Christ is going to take us. It's an adventure. One thing is for sure, we will be judged even by those who are Christians. Why? We are judged because God works in each of us differently. When God is working in us in a way which is unconventional, and someone doesn't understand, they typically judge us. This is something we all can learn from and sustain from judgment. We could inquire which may be more productive.

If we find ourselves being judged or judging, it is good to remember Matthew 7:1, "Do not judge, or you will be judged." Or, better yet, Luke 6:37-38 which states, "Do not judge, and you will not be judged. Do not condemn, and you will not be condemned. Forgive, and you will be forgiven. Give, and it will be given to you. A good measure, pressed down, shaken together and running over, will be poured into your lap. For with the measure you use, it will be measured to you."

Simply said, it is all because Jesus came to earth, died for our sins, rose on the third day and ascended into heaven with the Father that we now have our Comforter, our Counselor. The Holy Spirit works on our behalf to help us overcome our troubles in this world when we ask him for help. He also speaks to us. We are responsible to listen, and operate the power of the Spirit by speaking words or ideas of truth given to us by him. Because we are intelligent, we figure it out, even if it is not exact. It doesn't matter. God looks at our heart and our obedience.

Identifying Our Spiritual Battles

Some may say, "How do I know if there is really a spiritual battle going on in my situation." Well, we figure it out. Either we are not in right standing with God and need to get right with him and others or there could be a block in our movement forward. True, it may not be a spiritual battle. And, if it isn't a spiritual battle, it may be a miscommunication or something we don't understand. We are not on a witch hunt but rather need to have an awareness of the spiritual battles behind the scenes.

John 10:10 says, "The thief comes only to steal and kill and destroy; I came that they may have life, and have it abundantly." Let's face the facts. Our enemy doesn't want to do us any favors. He would rather steal our joy and our possessions, kill our relationships or us, destroy our mind or anything else we have opportunity to here on earth.

On the other hand, Jesus said he came so that not only would we have life but we could have it abundantly! Abundantly does not mean scraps. Nor does it mean we just get by with what we have. Jesus wants us abundant because we are his brothers and sisters. We are God's kids! Who are we going to serve? We make the choice by who we believe. The actions we take and the words we speak show whom we are following.

We will not be the tail, but rather the head, or the top of our life. We have this opportunity. When we know the rules to this game we call life, we know what we need to do to be successful.

When we are facing our giant problems which try to hinder us from moving forward, we can pray specific Scriptures placing our name in certain places or personalizing the verse. We can do this with many verses. For instance we could pray Isaiah 45:1-3 which says,

> This is what the LORD says to his anointed, to Cyrus, (insert our name) whose right hand I take hold of to subdue nations before him and to strip kings of their armor, to open doors before him so that gates will not be shut: I will go before you and will level the mountains; I will break down gates of bronze and cut through bars of iron. I will give you the treasures of darkness, riches stored in secret places, so that you may know that I am the LORD, the God of Israel, who summons you by name.

Remember, this is a spiritual battle. Our words move spiritual mountains when we speak them into being with trust in God and conviction from our hearts.

We could also pray Isaiah 54:17 which states, "… no weapon forged against you (me) will prevail, and you (I) will refute every tongue that accuses you (me). This is the heritage of the servants of the LORD, and this is their vindication from me,' declares the Lord."

We could also pray 1 John 4:4-6 or any other verse which speaks to us. When we personalize the Scriptures they become more real to us. We could also pray for God to bind the enemy and let our work proceed until finished. However we feel moved to pray in our mind and heart is how we should pray because every situation and person is different from another. This is where we can sit quietly and meditate on a specific Scripture, ask the Lord to speak to us, or just be quiet and listen for a moment. We may not know what to do in every situation. We may need to observe our surroundings and see what we think is best. If we don't know, it's good to wait. Ask God for help, then, listen to what he tells us.

We are intelligent. We have our minds to think through what might be best for us. Because we are intelligent we need to believe in ourselves enough to speak words we believe are correct and will help us through our situation. These are our affirmations. These affirmations just happen to be God's words to us. What we say out loud, our ears hear and we are able to believe those words more easily. These words we speak also help to move the spiritual mountains which hinder our forward movement.

If we are not moving forward in our struggle after speaking these words we may need to wait, or we may not be in right standing with God. If this is the case we can search our hearts, get right with God, then move forward in our situation and life. It really is that simple. We are the ones who have to be willing to look at ourselves, and speak God's words into the air.

When we truly believe Christ dwells in us we can operate our God given right to execute any spiritual battle which comes against us or between us and our God. When we operate our authority in Christ the force coming against us is therefore, inoperative. It cannot harm us. We may see chaos all around us but we feel peace inside our heart and soul. We eventually win the battle.

Each battle could be different from another. One thing for sure, when we feel the negative energy coming against us, and we stop it with our faith based words, spiritual forces are aware of us knowing about our power in Christ.

Although we have the authority to win our spiritual battles, we as Christians don't always exercise our authority. Why not? We may not know we can, or we may not know how. Or although we may know how to fight battles, we might feel weird about speaking words which express fighting spiritual battles. But speaking the words into existence is where we have electricity which turns on our lights, or in this case blasts our dynamite. The power is in our words.

Proverbs 18:21 says, "Death and life are in the power of the tongue and those who love it will eat of its fruits" (New American Standard Bible).

Because this is a change in our thinking, then behavior, we are sometimes resistant. If we understand this concept we know then that it is we who need to speak what we want done into being. We can't do this if we don't know or won't speak up. What we are fighting are spiritual battles so if we want to win, we must fight them in a way where we can win.

We have the power because the Bible says we have the power. It is up to us to believe and obey God, then act out our power with our words. We have reviewed some of the Scriptures which define our authority as Christians. There are plenty more but it does not matter if we don't either believe or operate them.

God does not change. When we are on God's side and speak out against evil or unrighteousness, we are helping God win the war against evil. We are also helping ourselves within our current situation, within our own community and within the body of believers.

When we pray we are asking God for his help. We ask him to help move the mountains out of our way so we can move forward in our life. It may take time, but we need to be patient and allow God to work things out in his timing.

When we fight these battles the way God intended us to fight, we are on his team. He is helping us win. However when we allow evil or unrighteousness to slide by us, we are not helping God's cause nor our own. We have the power and responsibility to remove our own spiritual mountains. Why? Because we are mature in Christ and know what to do about our situation. Not to do anything would be selfish in that we care more about what people think of us than what God thinks. If this is the case, it is possible a codependency issue needs to be addressed within ourselves. Or sometimes we are so tired, we give up our fight. If this is our case, it is unfortunate. We need to remember we can always ask for help.

What exactly does it mean when we read in Scripture, "… the glorious riches of this mystery, which is Christ in you, the hope of glory. We proclaim him, admonishing and teaching everyone with all wisdom, so that we may present everyone perfect in Christ. To this end I labor, struggling with all his energy, which so powerfully works in me."

The Spirit of God works in us and through us every day. This Holy Spirit whom Jesus referenced is the same Spirit whom hovered over the deep waters when the earth was without form and void in Genesis. When Jesus said, "... the time has come when true worshippers will worship God in spirit and in truth," this is partially what he was talking about. We are to take our place in the body of Christ and overpower our enemies so we can do what God has called each one of us to do. Does this mean we are always struggling with this spiritual battle? No! It means when we have issues, we may want to consider the spiritual side of the matter.

The book of Daniel references how Daniel had been praying for a very long time. However there was no movement forward because the Prince of Persia had blocked the archangel Gabriel from coming to Daniel's aid. The Prince of Persia was a spiritual being Gabriel had to overcome. Once the Prince of Persia had been taken down then Gabriel was able to come to Daniel's rescue. The same is true for us. We need to sometimes call in the big guns to help us move through a situation that is blocking our progress or movement forward.

We as Christians give up way too easily because we get frustrated. We are frustrated because we don't know we already won our battle. We are frustrated because we don't know how to fight our battle. We are frustrated because we allow other people to take over, or we are tired, or we just give up and lose our battles through our own forfeit. Ignorance is not always bliss.

We know what truth is, it is anything that is not a lie. Now it is time to operate the power of the Spirit in our lives. It is the combination of spirit and truth which makes our worship so powerful. We may not think fighting spiritual battles is worshiping God, but it is worship. It is because we are choosing who we believe and speaking it into the air.

Just as Eve was tricked, we have been tricked into not understanding how to utilize our authority in Christ. We may know to speak the truth but we don't know the power of our words. We will receive what we say. It's that simple. Now we need to use our words and see the results play out. What we put in our mind, we speak, then live out what we speak.

The Spirit of God is greater than what is in the world. We could use a revival from within our own souls. As the band, the Newsboys, sing in their song, "God's Not Dead" as the lyrics state:

> "He's living on the inside, roaring like a lion."

God is not dead and neither are we. God is alive. Christ is living on the inside of us and he is roaring like a lion wanting to get out! We are the ones who have free will to let the Spirit of God out of us or not. We have control over our lives to let that lion come out or suppress him.

Moving Mountains as a Nation

We have promises from God we need to proclaim with a loud voice when we undergo persecution. As we already know, one of our promises is, "No weapon formed against you shall prosper" (Isaiah 54:17a). As we stand firm on what the Word of God says, and proclaim our spiritual rights as a child of God, the devil and his kingdom has no legal right over us.

We as Christians are brow beaten by our pasts and by what others say or think that we can barely function. At times we can't help these worries from overtaking us. This therefore affects us as individuals as well as collectively within the body of Christ, and as a nation. We as a nation are suppressed because of our past decisions, our fallen economy, and our relationships. We know Scripturally we can overcome because, "greater is he who is in us than he who is in the world." But we as a nation need to stand up together in unity with this attitude. When we in fact believe this to be true we will begin to act on what we know and will see ourselves overcoming our problems in our daily situations and long term goals.

As we begin to speak and breathe life words into our daily situations, we begin seeing the life of our words being manifested. This is when we need to be vigilant in seeing our enemy come against us. He is a wise serpent and will use the words of others, even those closest to us, to try to rip us apart and get us to doubt. But we must also be wise as serpents, yet harmless as doves to move forward in what we know is right and true for ourselves. In fact, this is paramount because it moves spiritual mountains.

We were created for a purpose. We have cause to be here on this earth, not merely to exist, although, we do have that choice. Jeremiah 29:11 says, "For I know the plans I have for you, declares the Lord, plans to prosper you and not to harm you, plans to give you hope and a future." Even though God was talking to Jeremiah here, this is true for us today! When we allow God to guide us we are allowing him to fulfill his will in our lives which includes not harming us, but rather helping us prosper, giving us hope in a hopeless world and a future filled with abundance. Obedience, truth, and operating our authority in Christ doesn't sound too bad. That is unless we start to think we are unworthy, or it's too hard, or it's not for us, or we don't want to change our ways.

We are human. We as human's can only take so much. We might have a lot of fight in us but after five, ten or twenty years of fighting we get tired. At some point we need to ask ourselves if what we are fighting for is worth our energy and time. If we are staying where we are in life but want to move beyond our present situation then we need to change something.

God is a spirit which means he is not a physical being or in one place. He is not limited. He is omnipresent, meaning he is present everywhere. Therefore God can be worshiped anywhere, at any time. We can fight battles anytime, anywhere.

It does not matter where we worship that counts but how we worship. Being genuine is what God is looking for in his worshipers.

When Jesus said, "… true worshipers will worship God in spirit and in truth" he was saying there is a right attitude and a wrong attitude. He says, "Do you really want to worship me or not? Is your heart in it or not?" Jesus did not come to take away challenges necessarily, but rather to change us on the inside and empower us to deal effectively with problems from God's perspective. We do this throughout our week. Not just on Sunday.

This is a great honor to have Christ living in us, and to live out who we were created to be with the help of Christ. This is a privilege that we all have as born again Christians. This is our liberty in Christ. So many people have given up on God because they have been hurt, or did not feel loved or heard. They walk away because no one took the time to show them the way. Many come from broken families. As we allow Christ to shine in our lives, maybe just maybe, we can model this Christianity to some people who still seek God, his love and his acceptance. When we model overcoming obstacles, others may begin to believe they can overcome their obstacles.

When we adhere to the Christ inside of us, we can overcome all of the devils schemes. Some Christians really don't want to talk about the devil's schemes or Satan or Lucifer. But we need to know who we are dealing with on a spiritual level.

First John 4:4 is talking about the Christ in us versus the god of this world, the prince of the power of the air, Satan, who is that old serpent, the devil. He may have many names but his purpose is to deceive, kill, steal and destroy us. As he deceives us, we are allowing him to rule over our soul and our surroundings. It's time for us to take our stand and overcome him with the power and authority God gave us.

Because we are God's 'little children' we have overcome all of the devil's deceptions as we allow the Christ in us to take precedence. The Christ in us is our spiritual birthright as children of God. It is how we know we are born again, spiritually speaking. It is our deposit until Jesus comes back for his church. As children of God, we have a right to know our Father. When we allow the Word of God to live and breathe in our heart, we have the discernment needed to overcome our enemy's schemes, not just some of them. The Holy Spirit is constantly speaking to us. He is our Wonderful Counselor, and when we allow him to guide us, then greater is 'He' who is working through us, than he who is working in this world.

This is only one side of how the Holy Spirit works through us. We also have gifts of the Spirit. We will take a look at those gifts in our next chapter.

Audio and E-Books Play List Chapter 6:

Third Day—Born Again
http://www.youtube.com/watch?v=4m_dP2n-5W8

Natalie Grant—I Will Not Be Moved
http://www.youtube.com/watch?v=2wu8YM-XDvs

Flyleaf—All Around Me
http://www.youtube.com/watch?v=xN0FFK8JSYE

Newsboys—God's Not Dead
http://www.youtube.com/watch?v=S_OTz-lpDjw

Questions for Chapter 6

1. How has the Holy Spirit (God) been talking to you?

2. How have you been tempted to not do God's will?
3. How can you use your words to overcome your dilemma(s)?
4. What are five (5) goals you know God would like to see you accomplish?
5. Close your eyes and ask the Holy Spirit to reveal to you 3 steps per week you are able to take for each goal listed.
6. Visualize yourself accomplishing each step and each goal.

Spiritual Gifts

"Now about spiritual gifts, brothers, I do not want you to be ignorant."

1 Corinthians 12:1

As Jesus was ascending to the right hand of God he told his disciples to wait in Jerusalem until they received the gift of baptism from the Holy Spirit. As the disciples waited in Jerusalem for the gift, they were preparing for an annual event celebrated by Jews called Pentecost.

This event took place fifty days after the Passover, or what Moses called the "Feast of Weeks." Pentecost was originally celebrated for the harvesting of the spring crops but later the law given by God to Moses (Ten Commandments) was incorporated with the celebration of Pentecost. However, this particular year Pentecost had an additional meaning. On the day of Pentecost this year, about one hundred and twenty people were gathered together in an upper room in Jerusalem.

Eventually, just as Jesus said, the baptism of the Holy Spirit came. It came on the day of Pentecost. When the Holy Spirit came into the room the sound was "… like a blowing and violent wind which filled the entire house where they were sitting. They saw what seemed to be tongues of fire that separated and came to rest on each of them. All of them were filled with the Holy

Spirit and began to speak in other tongues as the Spirit enabled them" (Acts 2:1-4).

Throughout the book of Acts we read how men and women were baptized with the Holy Spirit. They not only spoke in tongues, but they prophesied, healed the sick, gave words of wisdom or words of knowledge. They dreamt dreams had visions, worked miracles and made history. There was no further record of the sound being like a violent wind, nor were tongues of fire noticed. Some scholars believe the initial sound and tongues of fire were the marks of entry of the Holy Spirit into our realm, and infusion into mankind.

Jesus said he would send the Counselor which is the Holy Spirit. When this happened the miraculous happened at the same time. They now had Christ working through them, just as we currently have Christ working through us as Christians.

The disciples of Jesus went from being known as Jewish followers of Jesus to Christians because they now had Christ working within them. This was due to the Holy Spirit making his entrance into the lives of these men and women on the day of Pentecost.

Today, some Christians who allow operation of the gifts of the Spirit are known as Pentecostals, Charismatic's, true worshipers or real believers. It doesn't matter what the label is, what matters is we are open to allowing the Holy Spirit work through us. We may not know the time or hour, it just happens throughout our day. It sometimes happens whether or not we are paying attention. So it is pretty exciting when we begin to notice.

Throughout the book of Acts we see thousands of people doing what Peter encouraged which was repenting, asking God for forgiveness of their sins then receiving the baptism of the Holy Spirit and speaking in tongues. It was that simple, and it is that simple for us today. When people believed and desired the gift of eternal life they also had an understanding as to the inclusion of the gifts of the Spirit. If they were not aware of the gifts of the Spirit, another disciple would make their way to them to help make them aware. Then they had the opportunity to receive. In retrospect, they received what they believed and desired to have. Again, the same is true for us today.

There was a turning point in Acts chapter 10 when Peter was given a vision to go to an Italian believer in God named Cornelius. He was a non-Jew otherwise known as a Gentile. Cornelius was a strong believer in God but could not worship in the temple because he was not Jewish. At this point Jews still did not associate with anyone outside their Jewish culture because they were not ceremonial clean according to the Jewish customs.

Although Peter questioned the Spirit of God's guidance to go to Cornelius, he went anyway as God showed him in a vision that nothing is impure if God has made it clean. In speaking with Cornelius, Peter realized God did not show favoritism. Instead, what he noticed was, God accepts all peoples from every nation who respect him and does what is right (Act 10:35).

While Peter was sharing the story of Jesus to Cornelius and his household they were all filled with the Spirit of God and began to speak in tongues. Peter was "... astonished that the gift of the Holy Spirit had been poured out even onto the Gentiles. For they heard them speaking in tongues and praising God" (Acts. 10:45).

The book of Acts was just the beginning of the workings of the Holy Spirit through Christians. In Acts chapter 9 we see the notorious killer of Christians, Saul of Tarsus, converted after he had given orders to kill Stephen. As Stephen was being stoned his last prayer request to God was for those stoning him to not have their sin held against them.

This is the account of the final moments of Stephen's life and what he said, "Meanwhile, the witnesses laid their coats at the feet of a young man named Saul. While they were stoning him, Stephen prayed, 'Lord Jesus, receive my spirit.' Then he fell on his knees and cried out, 'Lord, do not hold this sin against them.' When he had said this, he fell asleep" (Acts 7:58b-60). Now that is love cried out from Stephen's heart!

Could this possibly mean Stephen's prayer for their sin not to be held against them actually be the prayer which helped convert Saul, who later became the Apostle Paul? Paul did a complete turnaround. Instead of persecuting Christians he became one of the most influential Apostles of all time. He wrote several of the New Testament books and is credited for reaching out to the Gentile nations for their salvation. We may never know the full power of Stephen's last prayer. We do know that with God, all things are possible.

GIFTS TODAY

The Holy Spirit is still working through Christians today yet we do not hear much about the gifts of the Holy Spirit. There are many churches which acknowledge the gifts of the Spirit and operate them within their daily lives. There are other churches that believe in the gifts of the Holy Spirit but don't speak about them much publicly because they don't want to scare or offend people who are not familiar with the gifts. Sadly, there are also churches who believe these gifts no longer exist.

It would behoove us to remember God does not change. We change because we change our thinking. These gifts are still available to us today because we see them working through believers, and because God did not tell us otherwise. He wants to work through us because he wants us to prosper and be in good health. He wants us to win our battles and he wants to work through us to help others. He does not want us to allow ministry leaders to thwart their authority over us because of their unbelief or fear of the spiritual gifts. He wants us to be free to use them.

The gifts of the Spirit are spoken about throughout the New Testament. Some specific teachings are found in 1 Corinthians chapters 12-14. It is explained that although there are many types of gifts it is the same God at work through them. The first gift spoken of in 1 Corinthians chapter 12 is the gift for the common good.

This is interesting because we are all called to be, and do, good to others and the world around us. We see a lot of people insulting and not behaving respectfully toward other people. Although this may be the way of our culture it does not mean we have to conform to this way of thinking. Instead, we can conform to doing something good, or be respectful.

This is easy because we can feel how the Holy Spirit works through us. It feels good in our heart and soul when we help others or are respectful. At any rate, we don't feel guilty. We feel like we just want to help someone. Sometimes, it is us being kind because it is in our nature. Other times we feel the move of the Holy Spirit pushing us to help in a way that nudges us outside of our comfort zone.

After the first gift for the common good there are other gifts listed. Here is the continuing of the list: 2) Message of Wisdom; 3) Message of Knowledge; 4) Faith; 5) Gifts of Healing; 6) Miraculous Powers, or Miracles; 7) Prophecy; 8) Discerning or Distinguishing between Spirits; 9) Speaking in Tongues and; 10) Interpretation of Tongues.

Each of these gifts is distributed by the Holy Spirit to whomever he determines. Some people have operated all of the gifts and some have operated only one or two, it varies as to how the Spirit decides and how willing we are as Christians. We need to be aware of all of them and willing to operate them in order for the Holy Spirit to work through us.

We read later in chapter 12 how God has appointed a hierarchy within the body of believers, otherwise known as the church.

> Now you are the body of Christ, and each one of you is a part of it, and in the church God has appointed first of all apostles, second prophets, third teachers, then workers of miracles, also those having gifts of healing, those able to help others, those with gifts of administration, and those speaking in different kinds of tongues. *(I Corinthians 12:27-28)*

When we have these gifts they feel natural to operate them because they are our God given abilities. It feels good to operate within our own abilities. On the other hand, if these are not our gifts, they feel unnatural, like we are trying to make something happen instead of allowing it to flow through us. It feels stressful when we are not working within our gifting. Many of us have felt the pressure of being in a job in which we do not like. It is stressful and there is no joy. This is very similar.

It is possible for some believers to operate all of these functions but the point really is that everyone in the body of Christ has at least one of these functions. We just need to find out what we do best and do it to the best of our ability. This does not mean necessarily only in a church building. We are the body of Christ and the church is the body of believers. We therefore operate these gifts wherever we find ourselves. We could be at home, or working for a corporation, or helping at a school. We don't stop being available to God because we are not in a church building. Although, when we are in a church building surrounded by the body of Christ, sometimes our gifts become clear to us and we desire to give of ourselves within the organized church. This is good because all churches can use some good help, especially when we know we are gifted in a certain area.

Romans 12:6-8 is one Scripture passage listing gifts which many organized churches use to help educate their attendees in regard to serving within their church. Again, this Scripture is a list of gifts given to the body of Christ, not necessarily to only an organized church. This list is as follows:

> We have different gifts, according to the grace given us. If a man's gift is prophesying, let him use it in proportion to his faith. If it is serving, let him serve; if it is teaching, let him teach; if it is encouraging, let him encourage; if it is contributing to the needs of others, let him give generously; if it is leadership, let him govern diligently; if it is showing mercy, let him do it cheerfully.

Some people know what their gifts are and some do not. There is no need to take tests to find out what our gifts are but some people find them helpful. There are many spiritual gifts analysis tests available on-line or within our own churches. If it is a real matter of concern it is a good idea to see where we test out. Testing often confirms what we already know about ourselves and these days, everyone can use a little confirmation.

It is important to remember the Holy Spirit can do whatever he wants. Just because we test high in a certain area doesn't mean he can't use us in a different area. Our job is to be available and enjoy the journey along the way. We will always have interesting opportunities along the way of life if we remain open to serving God wherever he leads us. At the same time, people are not the Holy Spirit. We need to be able to discern whether God is working within us or if someone just needs our help. Either way, it's okay to help.

The gifts of the Spirit are fascinating to say the least. When we are used by God we feel good inside and know we help the kingdom of God each time he works through us. The more open we are to God using us in this way, the more we will be used, and blessed.

The book of Ephesians is another book speaking specifically in regard to gifts. In this case Jesus is being referenced in giving gifts to men, or more specifically, mankind. Women are included because there is no favoritism in the family of God. We are all "sons" of God through faith in Christ Jesus and therefore have Christ living within us. "There is neither male nor female for you are all one in Christ Jesus" (Galatians 3:28).

The gifts given in Ephesians are referenced by some as being the "Five-Fold Ministry." This labeling was given by ministries in regard to one person having the capability of having all five of these gifts listed. Although true, it is also possible for some people to only have one gift, or maybe two. Again, we cannot limit the Spirit of God and what he wants to do with someone who is willing to be a worker together with him.

Ephesians 4:11 says,

> It was he (Jesus) who gave some to be apostles, some to be prophets, some to be evangelists, and some to be pastors and teachers, to prepare

God's people for works of service, so that the body of Christ may be built up until we all reach unity in the faith and in the knowledge of the Son of God and become mature, attaining to the whole measure of the fullness of Christ.

This is quite the proclamation! First we have the hierarchy of the leadership within the body of Christ (body of believers worldwide). It then describes the leaders are to prepare the people for works of service, enabling them to know their gifts so the body can be strong structurally. With a strong understanding of who we are in Christ, we know our place in the body of believers. This helps us all continue to grow structurally stronger within the unity of our faith and knowledge of Jesus, the Son of God. With this strong structure of faith we become mature Christians. We are then able to attain the whole measure of the fullness of Christ because of our strength as one unit. We know this truth, believe it and act as a child of God operating the gifts and activating the Christ in us as we need. This is powerful!

We all have so many ideas and thoughts about how we think Christianity should look. Yet, Ephesians 4:2-3 says, "Be completely humble and gentle; be patient, bearing with one another in love. Make every effort to keep the unity of the Spirit through the bond of peace." What this says is it is possible to keep the unity through the bond of peace. It takes effort, humility, patience, gentleness and love. We may disagree on some issues as to how to run an organized church, but we can agree on the main ingredients of the body of Christ. This shows maturity whereby we can proceed to attaining the whole measure of the fullness of Christ.

Even though this may appear to be a difficult task for some, it is our duty to do our part because we chose to be in this family of God together. If we don't we miss out on our blessings and the furthering of the kingdom of God. Being in alignment with God is exciting. It is a journey throughout this time we have here on this earth. At the same time, we have more fun at living our lives out together, in alignment with each other, in unity of the Spirit.

We have more fun living and loving our lives when we love Jesus and his ways. Why put ourselves through anything other than chasing after Jesus? He loves us. He will never leave us or forsake us. He died for our sins so we can be with him throughout eternity. Why not give him our life, our attention? Why not trust the one who gave his life for us even though we did not promise him a thing? We could leave a legacy or we could have enjoyment seeing what God can do through us. Either way, we win!

Audio and E-Books Play List Chapter 7:

Casting Crowns—Voice of Truth
http://www.youtube.com/watch?v=tcuiuIwtpa4

Francesca Battistelli—Free To Be Me
http://www.youtube.com/watch?v=EKSQjSdU8VA

Josh Wilson—I Refuse
http://www.youtube.com/watch?v=6B1Lv8k5pEc

Brandon Heath—Give Me Your Eyes
http://www.youtube.com/watch?v=P5AkNqLuVgY

Questions for chapter 7

1. Do you know your spiritual gift(s)?
2. Have you operated your spiritual gift(s) in the past?
3. Would you be interested in taking a spiritual test assessment?
4. How do you feel about speaking in tongues?
5. Are you open to the possibilities of what God wants to do through you?

LOVE
THE BOND OF
PERFECTION

"God is Love."

1 John 4:16b

"And God said, 'Let us make man in our image, in our likeness, and let them rule over the fish of the sea and the birds of the air, over the livestock, over all the earth, and over all the creatures that move along the ground.' So God created man in his own image, in the image of God he created him; male and female he created them."

Genesis 1:26-27

In the beginning of time here on earth God showed us he is not a singular God. God said, "Let us make ..." He did not say, "Let me make ..." He was clearly including at least one other person or being. He could have been talking to someone else as well. But if he is saying, "let's make man in our image," he is including the same image of the one or one(s) to whom he is speaking.

In Genesis 1:2 it says, "... and the Spirit of God was hovering over the waters." So we know God is Spirit. Since we were created in God's image, we know we too are spirit. Our spirit is encased within our body. Since God said, "Let us make ..." we see God can think and craft something. We too can think and craft something. We may not be able to create the heavens and an earth but we can craft something out of what we have available to us. We can think and do something. In fact, we were made to think and do something.

God also showed he made man plural. After God said, "Let us make man in our image, in our likeness," he then said, "... let them rule over ..." he later said, "So God created man in his own image, in the image of God he created him; male and female he created them." Clearly God was talking about mankind not just one man. Mankind was to rule over the earth. This included both the males and the females together. After the fall, things changed. The woman's desire was now for her husband and the man ruled over his wife. Then Jesus came to earth as our Savior. He came and died for us, rose again on the third day, then he returned to the Father. Now we are not to consider necessarily being male or female but we are to consider each other as one in Christ when it comes to spiritual matters. (Galatians 3:28). In other words, as Christians, we are equal in Christ.

With this understanding we move forward in being who God has created us to be. We do this by allowing Christ to live through us and we support the same in everyone else within our family, both male and female. God does not want us to fight over the little things but rather love and respect each other. He wants us to be in unity in our understanding. He wants us to support each other so we can be built up in the body of Christ. We need to do this together. And when we do, we are a powerhouse kingdom for God because God rules our hearts individually and as a corporate unit.

GIFT CLARITY

There are some gifts given to the body of Christ which we could use a better understanding about. We need to know about them so we can choose if we want to utilize them in our daily walk. Worshiping God is not about going to church every Sunday as some may think. Being a faithful Christian is allowing Christ to work through us no matter where we are, what day of the week it is, or what time it is during the day. Being a Christian is being a child of God and therefore being ready to do whatever our Dad asks us to do for him. It is a parent-child relationship.

Knowing this we need to be aware of who God is and what tools he has given us to use to help him and his kingdom here on earth. We know God is a Holy Spirit. God is also light, omnipresent, omniscient (all knowing), and he is love. We are created in his image so we have the same characteristics as our Dad in heaven. This does not mean we are God by any means. We can look around us to see we are not God for several reasons. First, we don't love each other all the time. We don't know everything, even though we may think we do. And even though we can think and pray for someone, feel their presence even if they are half way across the globe from us, we are not physically there with them as is God. We may bring light into a room but we are not light per se'. The Christ in us is the light. We have the characteristics of God. There are also ways to grow in all of these characteristics.

First Corinthians 13:1 says, "And now I will show you the most excellent way. If I speak in the tongues of men and of angels, but have not love, I am only a resounding gong or a clanging cymbal." In other words, without love in our lives, it doesn't matter if we operate the gift of speaking in tongues. Speaking in tongues is one of our prayer languages to God and helps us to grow closer to him. But without love, we are noise makers. We may be able to move spiritual mountains with our prayers and words of faith, we may be able to prophesy a million times or take part in healings and miracles. Simply said, without love, we are nothing in God's eyes. God is love and if we are made in God's image, and are his kids, we too can show this characteristic in our life. In fact, it is most important to God, our Daddy in heaven.

This is not to say speaking in tongues and miracles and prophesies are not good. Those are all good. They build up the body of believers and speaking in tongues builds us up as individuals. We need to perform the gifts of the spirit in our lives to help ourselves and others remain strong in the faith and spiritually. But love is far greater than them all.

The book of Jude may be small but it is impactful. It is an exhortation in regard to preserving our faith and watching out for those who may try to persuade us to go off course. Although we will have people who will try to divide the body of Christ with harsh words, grumbling and finding fault, their motives stem from their own desires as they will boast about themselves and flatter others for their own advantage. In other words, they manipulate for their own benefit. We are not to be this way but rather be aware of those who try to trick us in these ways.

Jude 20-21 says, "But you, dear friends, build yourselves up in your most holy faith and pray in the Holy Spirit. Keep yourselves in God's love as you wait for the mercy of our Lord Jesus Christ to bring you to eternal life." Jude was the brother of Jesus and James. So he saw first-hand what can happen within the mind-set of believers. He saw how we as Christians are human and therefore need to stay strong in our faith. Part of this is speaking out against heresy, which is simply speaking the truth about a situation, or our faith. Another part of this is praying in the Holy Spirit, or in tongues.

Jude is saying there are two things which are the most important in this spiritual battle of ours. He is saying to build ourselves up in the faith by speaking in tongues and keep ourselves in God's love until eternity. But Paul says in 1 Corinthians 13:1 that love overrides speaking in tongues. This makes sense because God is love and he wants us to love others. However, we need to keep strong in our faith so we can love. With those of us who operate the gift of speaking in tongues, Jude is saying, do it a lot! Why? We speak in tongues because we are going to need to remain strong in the faith to rise above our circumstances.

We don't hear much about speaking in tongues, but it appears it is one of our biggest allies in the faith. When we speak in tongues our spirit is speaking mysteries to God. That in itself sounds powerful. Although we read that if we speak in tongues of men and of angels but don't exercise love then we are just a noise maker. We like to hear ourselves speak. At the same time, speaking in tongues is what is being measured against the power of love.

If speaking in tongues is one of the gifts given to us by the Spirit of God it must be useful. If 1 Corinthians 14:5 says, "I would like every one of you to speak in tongues," would this not mean that God, or at the very least Paul, wants all of us to speak in tongues? Or know it's possible? And if 1 Corinthians 14:2 says, "… anyone who speaks in a tongue does not speak to men but to God." Wouldn't we want to do that in our personal prayer life? And if 1 Corinthians 14:4 says, "Indeed, no one understands him; he utters mysteries with his spirit … He who speaks in a tongue edifies himself …" We might want to pay attention just a bit as who would not want to be instructed, educated or enlightened in the things of God? We are afraid of things we are not sure of and when we have spiritual leaders leading us away instead of toward such a gift then we are cautious. Yet, if we do not look into this matter which is measured against love, we may be missing out on something special God would like us to know.

If speaking in tongues means our spirit is speaking mysteries to God, would this not increase our likeness of God? Would this not give us insight into mysteries within our own lives and possibly others? Would this not increase our love? The answer to these questions is, yes. At the same time, if we are not making an effort to love our brothers and sisters in Christ more than we are speaking in tongues, we are not being who God wants us to be as a Christian. We therefore need to balance our use of the gifts and our time with God and that of helping others. This is what Jesus did. He spent time with God in the morning and then did his work throughout the day. It is similar for us as well.

How to Love

Let's face it, people are hurting and we have the tools to help them. That is what our Heavenly Father wants from us. When we help others we are showing God we love him. It is showing others we love them. It is out of the overflow of love in our hearts that we want to help others. It shows we are God's kids.

John 14:23 tells us what Jesus told his disciples; "If you love me, you will obey my teaching." What are his teachings? His commands and teachings are to love one another and to do the will of the Father.

Jesus came to fulfill the law, and he did so by laying down his life for us. He obeyed the Father. This is love. We are to lay down our lives for each other. What does this mean? We could start by laying down our pride, selfish ambitions, bitterness, and our old ways of thinking. We could forgive just like God forgives. And yet, he also forgets our sins. This is walking in love. We lay down our old ways of thinking that only bring us more sorrow, for the love and glory of God. This is the God kind of love. This is agape.'

When we walk in love, we don't want to steal, lie, or covet. In fact, it is very hard for us to do such things because we are not comfortable with these actions. We feel guilt if we do them. Why, because these things are the opposite of love. They are contrary to the Spirit of God. When we are walking in love, God is first because God is love. The Old Testament laws were for those who did not have the Holy Spirit ministering truth to their hearts and minds as we do. They didn't have the privilege of having the Holy Spirit guiding them on a daily basis. They needed to have direction and laws to follow because they did not have the same privileges we have as sons and daughters of God.

Now, there is a greater law. This greater law is the law of love. This law of love is gratefulness from us so that we love God with all of our heart, soul, mind, and strength, and love our neighbor as our self. This is the law God puts in our minds and writes upon our hearts. If we obey this law, our hearts do not condemn us. We do not feel guilt or shame about something we did. This is the law Jeremiah the prophet spoke about. We activate these thoughts by being obedient to them. We are obedient to them because we know, trust, and love God and his ways. Our faith works through the love we have for God. This is the love of God which transcends and has been poured into our hearts by the Holy Spirit.

Romans 5:5, "Now hope does not disappoint, because the love of God has been poured out in our hearts by the Holy Spirit who was given to us."

Realistically, we don't always want to love our neighbor or our brother or sister in Christ because they may have hurt us or, we just don't like them. But even Jesus said to turn the other cheek and if our enemy is hungry or thirsty give them what they need. This is love.

God forgives us every day when we sin against him. That is what he wants us to do with others. This kind of forgiveness is activated by our faith which works through the love of God poured into our hearts by the Holy Spirit. When we make choices out of the law of love we are living righteously in God's eyes. When we live righteously in Gods eyes we show our love toward him. Love suffers long. Love never fails.

1 Corinthians chapter 13 is one of the most popular chapters used during wedding ceremonies because it is known for its love characteristics. We may be in love with one another when we get married, but problems arise because we live in a fallen world and no one is perfect.

1 Corinthians chapter 13 also shows the maturity of a Christian. It is interesting how it shows up in the middle of the gifts of the Holy Spirit. It could be our mantra. One thing for sure is, "Love never fails …" (1 Corinthians 13:8). Yet prophecies fail, tongues will cease and knowledge will vanish because we only know partially what is really going on in our world around us. This is how it remains until Jesus returns for his Church, the body of believers. Because we know these things now we are called to be mature in what we know.

"When I was a child, I spoke as a child, I understood as a child, I thought as a child; but when I became a man, I put away childish things. For now we see in a mirror, dimly, but then face to face. Now I know in part, but then I shall know just as I also am known." But until that time of Jesus' return, we are to hold on to three very important things that cannot be seen by the naked eye but rather lives within each of our souls. "And now abide faith, hope, love, these three; but the greatest of these is love" 1 Corinthians 13:13.

Love gives our faith power. As we choose to do our part in walking in, and practicing love, nothing is blocking our prayer life, and whatever we ask for, we receive. When we do our part, God does his part because love never fails. This is our hope. This is a very powerful promise from our Heavenly Father who is Love, who is Spirit, who is the author and finisher of our faith.

First John 4:7-9 says, "Beloved, let us love one another, for love is of God; and everyone who loves is born of God and knows God. He who does not love does not know God, for God is love. In this the love of God was manifested toward us, that God has sent His only begotten Son into the world, that we might live through Him."

This is a choice we all have. We have an opportunity to live through the love of Jesus Christ. The same love that he loved us with while he was hanging on the cross for us. As born again believers we are called to love one another like Jesus loved us in that very crucial and powerful moment in time. When we do, we get to be a part of God's power and his love.

THE POWER OF FORGIVENESS

When our children lie to us or take something that is not theirs, we discipline them by letting them know what they did was wrong. Now they have awareness. If they lie or take something again, we will either tell them again, or take a privilege away from them, depending on their age. If they say they are sorry, we forgive them, and we forget about what they did. When our children are seven we do not typically remember what they did wrong at age four. When our children are twelve, we do not hold them accountable for what they did at age nine.

This is how God forgives us, and how he wants us to forgive others, and our selves. When he forgives, he forgets! This is the God kind of love that has been poured into our hearts. It may not be that simple for us as we are human, not gods. However, we can attempt to apply this rule because we also have Christ working in us. We are created in God's image, so it is possible to at least forgive or he would not have asked us to do so.

Some people have said they will forgive, but they will not forget. But this is not the attitude or love of God. We know this because God literally forgets our sins. It is we who remember our past sins and those of others. It is possible we remember because we have not forgiven ourselves. If we happen to remember a sin, we simply do not hold it against the person if they have already dealt with it. If they have not dealt with their sin we simply pray for them. We are new creations in Christ Jesus, yet we all make mistakes and we need to remember our own frailties. At the same time, we may not forget because God did not ask us to forget. He asked us to forgive. We have a memory which means we hold on to things at some level. What we are asked to do here is not hold a grudge. When we remember, we could just learn from the situation so we don't recreate it.

When Jesus died on the cross for us, he bore all of our sins for us. This means he forgave us before we asked him for forgiveness. Now, our Heavenly Father forgives us for our sins and unrighteous behaviors when we repent and ask for forgiveness, because Jesus paid the price for us. God loves us so much and sees our frailty so clearly that he knew we needed a Savior. He gave his only Son so we could live with him throughout eternity, if we choose. He did this because he loves us. This is the love of God poured into our heart. It is sacrificial.

> Therefore, as God's chosen people, holy and dearly loved, clothe yourselves with compassion, kindness, humility, gentleness and patience. Bear with each other and forgive whatever grievances you may have against one another. Forgive as the Lord forgave you. And over all these virtues put on love, which binds them all together in perfect unity. Let the peace of Christ rule in your hearts, since as members of one body you were called to peace. And be thankful. Let the word of Christ dwell in you richly as you teach and admonish one another

> with all wisdom, and as you sing psalms, hymns and spiritual songs with gratitude in your hearts to God. And whatever you do, whether in word or deed, do it all in the name of the Lord Jesus, giving thanks to God the Father through him.
>
> Colossians 3:12-17

This could be another mantra of ours.

Simply put, as children of God we need to forgive others, saved and unsaved. This is the start of us becoming more and more like Jesus. This is us having liberty in Christ. When we forgive, our heart does not condemn us, and we can go boldly to the throne of God with our prayer requests. Why do we know this is true? Because Jesus said,

> I tell you the truth, if anyone says to this mountain, 'Go, throw yourself into the sea,' and does not doubt in his heart but believes that what he says will happen, it will be done for him. Therefore I tell you, whatever you ask for in prayer, believe that you have received it, and it will be yours. And when you stand praying, if you hold anything against anyone, forgive him, so that your Father in heaven may forgive you your sins.
>
> Mark 11:23-24

If we are not forgiving someone, we are not walking in love because love forgives. This is a free-will choice which is ours alone. We choose our destiny with these types of decisions.

First John 2:9, "Anyone who claims to be in the light but hates his brother, (chooses not to forgive) is still in the darkness. But whoever loves his brother lives in the light, and there is nothing in him to cause him to stumble. But whoever hates his brother is in the darkness and walks around in the darkness; he does not know where he is going, because the darkness has blinded him."

We stumble in our decision making as well as spiritually because we haven't made our hearts right with others and therefore we are not right with God. This includes any judgments or prejudices we have towards others. We may not understand what is going on around us or inside of us because of this darkness. We may have confusion, and God is not the author of confusion. So when we have confusion it is good to ask God for clarification, or wisdom.

James 1:5 tells us, "… if we lack wisdom, ask God who gives it to us liberally, without finding fault." We are blind sometimes and don't even know it, but we feel miserable. This is our red flag. If there is any hate in our heart it has blinded us from seeing the hate and possibly the truth in the matter. When this happens we could get honest with ourselves and our creator. We could ask for wisdom to see through our pain. We need to see through the pain so we can identify what might not be right in our hearts. Then to make things right in our hearts, we need to do whatever is necessary to get right with God and anyone else. This purifies us.

Let's look at some facts. The opposite of love is hate. God is not hate. He is love. Satan on the other hand is here to kill, steal, and destroy us. Satan and his kingdom are filled with hate. If we choose not to forgive, we are allowing the devil's kingdom to work through us. It's not a pretty picture, but it is the spiritual reality. We may not want to look at the spiritual reality of our surroundings, and that is fine. However, it doesn't make it go away.

If we choose to hold grudges and therefore refuse to forgive, we have opportunities stolen from us, and we are slowly destroyed because our heart condemns us. We know forgiveness is the right thing to do, but we choose to allow our bitterness to get the best of us. Forgiveness is not only for the one we are forgiving. Forgiveness is ultimately for us. It gives us freedom from their power over us. This type of thinking is then passed on to our future generations. We choose our legacy.

Getting Real & Honest

We need to get real with ourselves and get honest with God. He knows our innermost thoughts and our heart anyway. We can't fool God even if we tried. We might be able to fool others, but again, we are only hurting and fooling ourselves. This is pride and arrogance on our part. It is also ignorance. If we simply ask God to show us what is causing this reoccurring sin or pattern in our lives, he will show us. Notice how he so graciously and lovingly shows us? This is how we are to reveal and restore others, in love and with grace.

Being made free is a choice, and a process. It sometimes takes us months, or even years to be comfortable in walking in God's love. Why, because we are constantly taking off the layers of our old ways of thinking. We are constantly renewing our minds, and we are constantly purifying our hearts with the Word of God, prayer, and the Holy Spirit's move in our lives. It takes work!

It's like taking the layers off of a raw onion, it stinks, and sometimes we cry uncontrollably. Yet as we begin taking off the most obvious front layers by being honest, then we begin to see other layers that need to be dealt with as well. As we continue in prayer and in God's Word, truth is revealed to us. As we continue peeling off the layers by making the changes necessary, we begin feeling freedom from our past sins, and we begin enjoying our liberty in Christ. We begin loving life more fully because our choices are God centered and we don't want to hurt ourselves or others anymore.

Jesus said to love your neighbor as yourself. He also said love your enemy. This means we regard everyone as a person. We may not like them, but we still respect them. This may be God's grace working through us. It is also common sense. This may be God's mercy working through us, but it most certainly is humane. God is in the humanity business. So, anyway we want to look at it, it is God's love working through us.

Galatians 5:22 says, "The fruit of the Spirit is love." If we love God, we will obey his commandments. We will be firm in what we know, and we will be protected from our enemy. As we live our lives as the children of love we also have joy, peace, patience, kindness, goodness, faithfulness, gentleness and self-control because these are all fruits of the Spirit. Against such, there is no law (Galatians 5:22-23). This is powerful in that our freedom in Christ is unexplainable. We feel the move of the Spirit and we feel the joy overriding the chaos around us as we continue to do what we know is right in a situation. God wins. We win. The body of Christ wins. And many more are brought into the kingdom of God because they see God working through us.

The body of Christ has an opportunity here to glorify God in their obedience, and enjoy all of the perks that come with obedience. As we abide in Jesus' words we will have peace that is unexplainable. We are his disciples. We are disciplined and we will be ready to tell anyone about Jesus, or God or the gospel whenever anyone asks whether we feel like it or not. Why? Because the Holy Spirit is always pouring the love of the Father into our hearts and giving us words to say. We don't have to wonder what we will say when anyone asks. In fact, when someone asks a question about God, if we don't know, we can quietly ask God in our mind to give us a response. While we are listening for the answer in our mind, the Holy Spirit speaks. Then we respond with the answer. If we have not done this before, it may take practice. It is quite interesting though how the Holy Spirit is never late; he is right on time. Therefore, we are right on time with our response.

We have to let go of our need to be in control of everything and everyone else around us. We simply need to do our part, and continue to trust God will do his part. As we follow his directions, we don't have a need to control the outcome, we simply continue on our path with him. This is our freedom in Christ.

Abounding Love

Philippians 1:9-11 says, "And this is my prayer: that your love may abound more and more in knowledge and depth of insight, so that you may be able to discern what is best and may be pure and blameless until the day of Christ, filled with the fruit of righteousness that comes through Jesus Christ, to the glory and praise of God."

This is huge! We see our love is to be filled to over flowing more and more in knowledge, insight and discernment. We do this by walking in God's love, and practicing our Biblical knowledge. The more we know and practice God's ways, the more discernment and love we will have because we have greater understanding. It is therefore easy for us to speak of those things that are right and excellent because we have confidence in our Lord and in the Spirit's words to us.

As we humbly speak with sincerity, we are without offense because we have done what is right. If others around us are offended, it's because what we have said or done has touched a part in them that needs healing. If what we say convicts another, we need to stay firm in how the Holy Spirit is guiding us. Our job is to simply speak and do God's will, and let the Holy Spirit take over from there in our lives and in the lives we touch. This life is adventurous and fun because of the freedom. At the same time, life can be a challenge because not everyone is comfortable with change. We therefore need to give people their space to process the new information.

We help to set the captives free by teaching the gospel. Teaching may not be our gift, but remember, God can use us however he chooses. It's up to us to allow him to work through us. Part of teaching is being a good example. We teach perfect love, not judgment, casts out fear. We teach God has not given us the spirit of fear, but of power, through the Holy Spirit; love, through our Heavenly Father; and a sound mind, through Jesus Christ our Lord who is the written Word of God and Christ within us.

As we continue to believe, and therefore continue to do what the Word of God says, we will continue to cast the fear out of our lives, and our faith is strengthened. As we love others with sincerity, we help to cast the fear and doubt out of their lives. Why? Because the perfect love flowing through us, is from God. This includes confronting or exposing sin in the lives of others. We do this by speaking the truth in love and allowing the Spirit to move through us.

We begin to be made freer in our liberty in Christ because our selfish ways are being replaced by the love of God. We begin to understand the meaning of being a new creation in Christ, and our old ways of thinking leave because we have greater spiritual awareness and understanding. We enjoy making better choices in our life, and we are very careful in regard to what we allow ourselves to say, do, and think.

We are the salt of this earth, we have the love of Jesus inside of our hearts, and we are all beautifully and wonderfully made. We are marvelous in God's sight and we need to believe in our hearts that we are his children.

We need to believe that God has not given us the spirit of fear, but of power, love and a sound mind. We need to rise above all of the chaos around us, proclaiming what is ours, and being who God has created us to be in Christ! We need to change our attitude to a more positive nature; speaking life-giving, positive, power-packed words.

We also need to thank our Heavenly Father for loving us like no other, and giving us his son, our Lord Jesus Christ, so we can live eternally with him. We need to give him thanks for giving us the opportunities of a lifetime here on earth, so we can rise above. "… For indeed the kingdom of God is within you" (Luke 17:21).

May God bless you as you embark upon your righteous walk with him.

Audio and E-Books Play List Chapter 8:

Rich Mullins—Creed
http://www.youtube.com/watch?v=QuqdvuQGXCU

Sidewalk Prophets—Live Like That
http://www.youtube.com/watch?v=GfosSggwQS0

Holly Starr—Don't Have Love
http://www.youtube.com/watch?v=E06cXUgI9_s

Newsboys—He Reigns
http://www.youtube.com/watch?v=_io6j1EytGA

Building 429—Where I Belong
http://www.youtube.com/watch?v=he32vwlKQPY

QUESTIONS FOR CHAPTER 8

1. Is there something holding you back from allowing the love of God to flow through you?
2. If so, what or who is it?
3. What is the first step you need to take to clear this from your slate?
4. Visualize yourself finishing the task of removing your obstacle.
5. Now, visualize you loving every family member, friend and neighbor.
6. Ask God to bring someone to your mind that He would like you to assist in some way
7. Ask God to show you what to assist.
8. Visualize yourself helping as God inspired you.

SCRIPTURES TO MEDITATE ON:

"But when the fullness of the time had come, God sent forth His Son, born of a woman, born under the law, to redeem those who were under the law, that we might receive the adoption as sons. And because you are sons, God has sent forth the Spirit of His Son into your hearts, crying out, 'Abba, Father!' Therefore you are no longer a slave but a son, and if a son, then an heir of God through Christ," Galatians 4:4-7.

"Therefore I also, after I heard of your faith in the Lord Jesus and your love for all the saints, do not cease to give thanks for you, making mention of you in my prayers: that the God of our Lord Jesus Christ, the Father of glory, may give to you the spirit of wisdom and revelation in the knowledge of Him, the eyes of your understanding being enlightened; that you may know what is the hope of His calling, what are the riches of the glory of His inheritance in the saints, and what is the exceeding greatness of His power toward us who believe, according to the working of His mighty power which He worked in Christ when He raised Him from the dead and seated Him at His right hand in the heavenly places, far above all principality and power and might and dominion, and every name that is named, not only in this age but also in that which is to come. And He put all things under His feet, and gave Him to be head over all things to the church, which is His body, the fullness of Him who fills all in all", Ephesians 1:15-23.

"Now we have received, not the spirit of the world, but the Spirit who is from God, that we might know the things that have been freely given to us by God," I Corinthians 2:12.

"Now hope does not disappoint, because the love of God has been poured out in our hearts by the Holy Spirit who was given to us." Romans 5:5

"Bless the LORD, O my soul; And all that is within me, bless His holy name! Bless the LORD, O my soul, And forget not all His benefits: Who forgives all your iniquities, Who heals all your diseases, Who redeems your life from destruction, Who crowns you with loving kindness and tender mercies, Who satisfies your mouth with good things, So that your youth is renewed like the eagle's." Psalm 103:1-5

"The law of the wise is a fountain of life, to turn one away from the snares of death," Proverbs 13:14.

"For by the grace given me I say to every one of you: Do not think of yourself more highly than you ought, but rather think of yourself with sober judgment, in accordance with the measure of faith God has given you," Romans 12:3

"Surely I have taught you statutes and judgments, just as the Lord my God commanded me, that you should act according to them in the land which you go to possess," Deuteronomy 4:5.

Agape',
Lu Ann

Britt Nicol—All This Time
http://www.youtube.com/watch?v=Z5PfWaMWBmA

For my little five-year-old within, He was walking with us all this time.